Commercial Agency

A Practical and Legal Guide

Oliver Segal QC – https://oldsquare.co.uk/people/oliver-segal-qc/

Oliver specialises in all fields of employment and discrimination law and in commercial agency law.

Within employment law he has particular specialist experience in: collective disputes (including industrial action, union recognition, TUPE and collective agreement cases); breach of contract claims (including restrictive covenants, PHI and negligent reference cases); and equal pay claims.

Oliver is the leading barrister within the field of commercial agency law; he acts for both agents and principals and has appeared in several of the most important cases, including the House of Lords case of *Lonsdale v. Howard & Hallam*. Other commercial agency cases include *Software Incubator Ltd v Computer Associates Ltd* (reference from Supreme Court to CJEU; CJEU hearing 2020); *Pluczenik Diamond Co NV v W Nagel (A Firm)* (2018) [2018] EWCA Civ 2640; *Alan Ramsay Sales & Marketing Ltd v Typhoo Tea Ltd* (2016) [2016] EWHC 486 (COMM); *Brand Studio Ltd v St John Knits Inc* (2015) [2015] EWHC 3143 (QB); *Charles Shearman (t/a Charles Shearman Agencies) v Hunter Boot Ltd* (2014) [2014] EWHC 47 (QB); *Crocs Europe BV v Craig Lee Anderson & Anor (t/a Spectrum Agencies (a partnership))* (2012) [2012] EWCA CIV 1400.

The directories say:

"He's an extremely good advocate." "He's spectacular in industrial action cases and extremely reliable. An enormous brain on legs." – Chambers & Partners 2021

"He understands the motivations and objectives of clients and that is very important. Oliver combines his extensive knowledge with a tenacious drive for a fair and just outcome. He is our go-to silk for industrial action." – The Legal 500 2021

Oliver is "exceptionally knowledgeable in his field, very client-focused,... very bright, and a great advocate." – Chambers & Partners 2019.

Ben Griffin – https://dwfgroup.com/en/people/b/ben-griffin

Ben is a Legal Director at DWF Law LLP, a global legal business. Ben specialises in complex, high-value, cross-jurisdictional litigation and arbitration, with a particular focus on Russia and the CIS. He has also developed a practice in commercial agency law.

The directories say:

"Ben Griffin is noted for his expertise in commercial agency disputes, and he has 'a deep knowledge and understanding of the case law in this field." – Legal 500 2019

Ben Griffin is a *"sharp and smart litigator"* – Legal 500 2021.

"Ben Griffin is focused, easy to work with and has excellent judgment as to where to focus on in a case." – Legal 500 2021.

"Ben Griffin has a growing reputation for his commercial litigation practice, which includes frequently acting for foreign nationals and high net worth individuals from Russia and the CIS. "Ben adds real value to any dispute," says a source, adding: "He is very committed to his clients, commercial in his approach, very thorough and strong on the law." – Chambers & Partners 2021

Commercial Agency
A Practical and Legal Guide

Oliver Segal QC, Old Square Chambers

Ben Griffin, DWF Law LLP

Law Brief Publishing

Published 2021 by Law Brief Publishing, an imprint of Law Brief Publishing Ltd
30 The Parks
Minehead
Somerset
TA24 8BT

www.lawbriefpublishing.com

Paperback: 978-1-913715-64-9

PREFACE

This book is written by the leading barrister and one of the leading solicitors in the field of the Commercial Agents (Council Directive) Regulations 1993 (the "**Regulations**"). But it is not a book written only for lawyers. The intention is to provide practical analysis and advice to agents, principals and their representatives (non-legal and legal) on the key questions that arise between them – during an agency relationship and following its conclusion.

When do the Regulations not apply? What rights and obligations do the parties have during the agency? What sort of (mis-)conduct entitles the other party to terminate for cause? How can an agent or principal vary the terms of the agency without ending it? When is an agent entitled to an indemnity or compensation following termination? How does one calculate the value of that indemnity or compensation?

These are questions that regularly concern agents and principals, to which they and their representatives need clear, non-legalistic answers if they are to avoid ending up facing each other in costly court proceedings. Indeed, strange as it may sound coming from lawyers, this book is designed to enable the avoidance of litigation as well as to assist in conducting that litigation. Of course, if parties cannot agree and the stakes are sufficiently high, the agent, the principal or both will want proper legal advice; but the aim of this book remains to enable a ready, practical understanding of the relevant issues, so that disputes can be avoided where possible or resolved quickly and sensibly where not.

As a result, this book is structured so that on each topic there is first a clear, non-legalistic explanation of the issues together with concise practical tips, followed by a detailed examination of what the Regulations say and how they have been interpreted by the courts.

The law stated in this book is accurate at 14 December 2020.

Note on Brexit

The Regulations were enacted into law because the UK was required to implement a European Directive on commercial agency.* They are not the independent product of the UK Parliament. The UK leaves the EU on 31 December 2020. However, most EU applicable law – including the Regulations – will remain in effect indefinitely until it is repealed or amended. Thus, at this stage, the only imminent potential impact of Brexit upon the application of the Regulations relates to contracts providing for an applicable law which is of a non-EU jurisdiction. This is discussed Chapter 3 below. It should also be noted that UK courts are not bound by decisions of the Court of Justice of the European Union ("CJEU") made after 1 January 2021, but they may have regard to such judgments. However, the UK courts will be bound by judgments of the CJEU made after 1 January 2021 which were pending before that date. This is particularly relevant to a commercial agency case currently pending before the CJEU which is discussed in Chapter 2. The UK courts – except the Supreme Court and Court of Appeal – remain bound by EU case law decided before 1 January 2021.

Oliver Segal QC
Ben Griffin
December 2020

* Council Directive of 18 December 1986 on the coordination of the laws of the Member States relating to self-employed commercial agents (86/653/EEC)

CONTENTS

CHAPTER 1
INTRODUCTION

Why were the Regulations introduced? What do they try to achieve?

The short answer to the first question is, the Regulations were introduced because an EU law (Directive) forced the UK to do so.

The short answer to the second question is, the Regulations try to achieve the purposes of the Directive agreed in Europe: to provide similar protections for commercial agents across the EU; so that principals in some EU countries (where agents had valuable rights) were not facing unfair competition from principals in other EU countries (where agents had no such rights).

History

The detailed history is not that important or interesting (except to those interested in EU politics and institutions, or the UK's relationship with the EU). In summary:-

1. There were well-established laws in both France and Germany – and to some extent Italy – which gave to commercial agents certain rights (many of them not dissimilar to some of the rights employees have), including a monetary entitlement if the principal caused the agency contract to be terminated.

2. At the instigation of those countries – and after 10 years of consideration, consultation and delays – the EU Directive was published in 1986, requiring all Member States to enact laws providing for similar rights to be granted to agents based in those various States. Most had to do so by 1990; the UK secured an extension to 1994.

3. Where the laws of the two main countries (France and Germany) were not consistent, the Directive either squared the circle, or (in relation to the termination payments) gave other Member States

the right to choose between them. The UK effectively passed on that choice to the principals and agents.

4. As may be gathered, the UK did not want to introduce the Regulations and legislated at the last possible moment (just before the deadline of the start of 1994) by simply copying out to a very great extent the EU Directive as the Regulations.

Primary features

Some of the features of the Regulations are not so different to what English law recognised in any event: the obligations of the agent to act in good faith; the right of the agent to be paid a typical rate for that industry if no rate is agreed.

However, the Regulations also create rights and obligations, which are unfamiliar to English law (some of which the principal and agent might have chosen to put into their contracts anyway), which principals and agents must adhere to (or in some cases, perhaps, must adhere to unless they specifically agree not to).

Those new mandatory rights and obligations are primarily:-

1. The principal must provide its agent with certain documents and information, including a written contract if asked (the agent too has to provide a written contract if asked by the principal – an unlikely event in practice).

2. An agent is entitled to commission on sales to customers s/he has introduced, or within his/her exclusive territory, even if s/he had nothing to do with the sale.

3. An agent is entitled to commission on post-termination sales where either the order arrives before termination, or where it arrives within a reasonable period afterwards and the agent won the order in practice.

4. An agent is entitled to commission on orders even if not fulfilled by the principal if the principal is to blame for that.

5. An agent is entitled to regular commission statements and to demand extracts from sales ledgers, etc., to check s/he is not being underpaid.

6. An agent is entitled to a minimum period of notice of termination (up to 3 months).

7. An agent is entitled to a payment on termination by the principal, or if s/he is forced to resign the agency by the principal's failure to stick to its contractual obligations, or if s/he is retires because of age or becomes too ill to continue.

Why are the Regulations so important?

It is those new mandatory rights that make the Regulations so important; the Regulations provide a raft of protections to the agent, the most significant of which (usually) being that set out at 7 above: when the principal terminates the agreement, when the agent retires, or can no longer work because of ill health, or dies, s/he (or their estate) is automatically entitled to a termination payment (under Regulation 17), which could be substantial.

Indeed, the protectionist stance of the Regulations should be borne in mind by the principal, agent and their advisers whenever they are considering their position.

Before the Regulations came into force on 1 January 1994, the principal/agent relationship was governed by longstanding English common law principles where freedom of contract was the watchword – meaning that parties to a contract could agree whatever they wished.

This meant that a sales agent could invest 20 years and significant effort building up a principal's brand only to see his contract terminated, leaving the principal free to walk away with the benefits created by the agent's work with the end customer. Unless the agent could establish a breach of contract by the principal causing the agent loss, he had little remedy. This led to one Judge referring to commercial agents as "*a down-trodden race*... [who] *need and should be afforded protection against their principals*"[1].

The Regulations marked a sea change in the law relating to agency in Great Britain. A failure to properly understand the new rights, and how the court approaches them, can be costly for agents and principals. Indeed, in one case under the Regulations, the Judge said "*the Regulations are dealing with concepts which are strange to English lawyers*".[2] As a result, this remains generally an all-too superficially understood area of law, even amongst lawyers.

The Regulations were enacted as a result of a European Directive requiring all EU Member States to adopt similar laws in relation to commercial agents.[3] Before the Directive, the law of commercial agency varied across the European community; so, for example, in England agents had no statutory protection, but in Germany they were well looked after. As explained in the Directive, its purpose was to:

1. further competition in the EU's common market;
2. harmonise the laws pertaining to commercial agents across the European Union; and
3. "*ensure a minimum level of protection for commercial agents*".[4]

The Directive (mostly) achieved the second purpose (though different member states implemented the Directive in different ways). On a practical level for agents and principals today, however, the most significant purpose is the third: that is, to prevent principals from abusing their dominant position over an agent and, upon termination, to give agents appropriate recompense for the goodwill that they create for their principals. In one case on the Regulations, the Judge explained: "*What the Directive is aimed at is the protection of agents by giving them a share of the*

1 *Page v Combined Shipping and Trading Co Ltd* [1997] 3 All ER 656, 660. In *Lonsdale (trading as Lonsdale Agencies) v Howard & Hallam Ltd (Winemakers' Federation of Australia Inc intervening)* [2007] UKHL 32, Lord Hoffman suggested that this statement was made "*with more than a touch of irony*".

2 *Tamarind v Eastern Natural Gas* 2000 WL 774929.

3 Council Directive of 18 December 1986 on the coordination of the laws of the Member States relating to self-employed commercial agents (86/653/EEC)

4 *Ingmar BG Ltd v Eaton Leonard Technologies Inc* (C-381/98) [2000] ECR I-9305.

goodwill which they have generated for the principal and from which the principal derives benefit after the agency agreement has been terminated…"[5].

5 *Tamarind v Eastern Natural Gas* 2000 WL 774929

CHAPTER 2A

WHAT IS A COMMERCIAL AGENT? A PRACTICAL GUIDE

In order to qualify for the protections set out in the Regulations, an agent must meet the definition of "*commercial agent*" in Regulation 2(1)[6], which provides:

> "*2(1) In these Regulations—*
>
> *"commercial agent" means a self-employed intermediary who has continuing authority to negotiate the sale or purchase of goods on behalf of another person (the "principal"), or to negotiate and conclude the sale or purchase of goods on behalf of and in the name of that principal...*"

When the Regulations came into force, principals sought to defeat agents' claims based on the argument that they did not have "*continuing authority to negotiate and conclude the sale or purchase of goods*" on their behalf. In a slew of cases the Courts found for the agents and interpreted Regulation 2 widely – on the basis that the Courts have to give effect to the purpose of the Regulations – which is to protect agents.

That said, principals have continued to run arguments that an agent is not a commercial agent on the grounds that they do not have continuing authority to negotiate. As a general rule, however, an agent is almost certain to be a commercial agent within the meaning of the Regulations if they:

1. are independent of the principal (they are not an employee, partner or group company of the principal); and

6 The fact that the Regulations apply "*in relation to the activities of commercial agents in Great Britain*" pursuant to Regulation 1(2) is considered below.

2. have authority to approach customers and market a principal's goods (not services), whether exercised regularly or not. As a general rule, in order to benefit from the Regulations, agents do not need to have authority to reach agreement on commercial terms or prices,[7] but simply to seek to build profile and customer base for the principal; and
3. are remunerated by commission (though they may also be remunerated by way of fixed retainer).

An agent is <u>not</u> a commercial agent if they:

1. Act as an officer of a company or association when binding that company or association (Regulation 2(1)(i));
2. Are a partner who is lawfully authorised to enter into commitments binding on his partners (Regulation 2(1)(ii));
3. Are an insolvency practitioner (Regulation 2(1)(iiii));
4. Are unpaid (Regulation 2(2)(a));
5. Operate on commodity exchanges or in the commodity market (Regulation 2(2)(b))[8];
6. Are Crown Agents for Overseas Governments and Administrations (Regulation 2(2)(c));
7. Are agents whose activities as commercial agents are to be considered secondary (Regulation 2(4)).
8. Act on their own account[9]. Distributors are not covered by the Regulations[10].

---

7 See, for example, *PJ Pipe & Valve v Audco India* [2005] EWHC 1904

8 What constitutes operating on commodity exchanges or in the commodity market was considered in *Pluczenik Diamond Co NV v W Nagel (A Firm)* [2018] EWCA Civ 2640, in which the authors acted for the successful claimant.

9 *AMB Imballaggi Plastici SRL v Pacflex Ltd* [1999] 2 All ER (Comm) 249.

10 This is the case in England although there are circumstances where distributorship agreements are affected by the Directive (for example in Germany) although that is outside the scope of this book.

9. Are sub-agents[11].

There is no need for an agent to have a written contract. Provided they perform the function of a commercial agent and meet the definition in Regulation 2, they will benefit from the protections contained within the Regulations.

---

11 *Light and others v Ty Europe* [2003] EWCA Civ 1238.

CHAPTER 2B

WHAT IS A COMMERCIAL AGENT? LEGAL GUIDE

Regulation 2

How the Courts have approached the definition of "commercial agent"

On the face of it, the definition at Regulation 2(1) is clear. But look more closely and it is fraught with ambiguity. Does the agent have to negotiate *and* conclude contracts? What does "*negotiate*" mean in this context? What do the Regulations mean by "*goods*"? What about agents who sell a principal's goods and services as a package? What does "*continuing authority*" mean?

As a result of these ambiguities, following the coming into force of the Regulations, Regulation 2 became an early battle ground between principals and agents, as principals sought to defeat claims by agents by arguing that they did not meet the definition and therefore could not benefit from the protections of the Regulations. The law is somewhat more settled now and principals should approach arguments that an agent is not a commercial agent under the Regulations with caution; the moral of the cases is that agents, if they are operating as a traditional sales agent, usually win this battle.

"Self-employed intermediary"

The phrase "*self-employed intermediary*", on the face of it, could mean that only individuals benefit from the Regulations. After all, how can a company be "*self-employed*"?

In *Bell Electric Ltd v Aweco Appliance Systems GmbH*,[12] it was argued, on behalf of the principal, that the term "*self-employed intermediary*" only applied to natural and not legal persons (i.e. did not apply to companies

---

12 [2002] EWHC 872

and other corporate entities). The Judge gave this argument short shrift, holding that the argument was "*wholly unsustainable*"[13], on the basis that the Directive upon which the Regulations are based refers to the need to remove restrictions on the freedom of establishment and the freedom to provide services, and it is clear that under European Union law, the rules relating to such principles apply both to legal as well as to natural persons.

As a result, it is beyond doubt that individuals, companies, partnerships, LLPs and other corporate vehicles all fall within the meaning of "*self-employed intermediary*". In this context, self-employed means, simply, that the agent is a distinct entity from the principal; the agent is, in effect, an independent contractor.

"Continuing authority"

In *Invicta v International Brands*[14], the court accepted the Claimant agent's submissions that whether an agent has continuing authority to negotiate within the meaning of Regulation 2(1) is to be determined at the time the agency agreement was made[15]. The court agreed that this means that provided an agent has authority at the outset of the relationship, it is immaterial if that authority comes to be exercised less frequently (or even not at all) as the agency continues and customer relationships are established and then cemented. The important factor is that the authority must not be withdrawn. From this, the appropriate question to ask appears to be: would the agent be acting beyond its authority by approaching potential customers? Unless the authority conferred at the start of the relationship has been withdrawn by the principal, the answer must surely be no, and the agent has the requisite continuing authority.

Whilst it was generally thought amongst practitioners that this issue was relatively clearly settled, in *W Nagel (a firm) v Pluczenik*[16] Mr Justice Popplewell found that:

---

13 [2002] EWHC 872 (QB) at paragraph 50.

14 [2013] EWHC 1564 (QB)

15 This was the approach adopted in *Tamarind International v Eastern Natural Gas Tamarind International Ltd v Eastern Gas (Retail) Ltd* Times 27 June 2000; [2000] Eur LR 708

16 [2017] EWHC 1750 at paragraph 43

> "*The relevant time at which to judge the nature and scope of the agent's retainer is in my view the date on which it is necessary to determine whether it is or is not a commercial agent for the purposes of the relief being claimed. In this case that is the date of termination because the remedies claimed (other than that under Regulation 7 which arises equally in contract at common law in any event) are consequent on termination or the position post termination.*"

This appears to give principals scope to argue that whilst an agent was a commercial agent at the outset of the relationship, by the time of termination it was no longer operating (and therefore engaged) as such and therefore should not obtain the post-termination benefits provided by the Regulations. However, it is important to note that *Nagel* was an unusual case where there was no written contract and where the issue at stake was not the scope of the agent's authority; the point the court was making was that where the terms of the contract changed over time (the agency had lasted several decades), the appropriate time to identify what the terms were was at the time of termination. In a more normal case, and particularly where there is a written agency contract, it will be difficult (though, if the facts support it, not impossible) for a principal to argue that the contract has been varied by conduct such that agent's authority has been revoked.

In *Poseidon Chartering BV v Marianne Zeeschip VOF and others,*[17] a Netherlands court asked the Court of Justice of the European Communities (CJEU) whether the concept of "commercial agent" extended to an independent intermediary who acted in the conclusion of a single contract, which was renewed annually, where that intermediary was involved in the process of annual renewal. The CJEU had no qualms in finding that the intermediary was a commercial agent, as the agent had authority not only in relation to the original contract, but in relation to its renewal.

Following these decisions, and in the light of the purpose of the Regulations, unless it is obvious that the agent should not have been acting on behalf of the principal (i.e. the principal had told the agent to

---

17 [2007] Bus. LR 446

desist contacting customers, or the course of conduct had been such that this could clearly be inferred), it appears that the question of whether the agent had continuing authority will be resolved in the agent's favour.

"the sale or purchase of..."

The key issue of note in relation to this part of Regulation 2 is that the Regulations apply not only to sales agents, but to agents who have continuing authority to negotiate the *purchase* of goods on behalf of their principal. Whilst buying agents are rare, they are commonplace in some sectors, such as the purchase of diamonds[18], and in the case of *Page v Combined Shipping*[19], the agent who acted for his principal buying and selling goods was held by the Court of Appeal to be entitled to compensation under the Regulations.

"To negotiate"... "or to negotiate and conclude"...

In the early days of the Regulations, principals often sought to defeat claims for post-termination payments on the grounds that their agents did not have authority to negotiate the sale or purchase of their goods, in the sense that the agents did not deal with customers in relation to prices or the terms of sale between principal and customer. The courts therefore looked into the meaning of "negotiate" in detail to assess whether an agent who promotes the principal's goods, presents price lists, builds a relationship with the customer and refers orders to the principal, but does not have authority to bind the principal or negotiate price, could be said to be "negotiating". As a result, there are a number of reported cases in which judges have considered what the word "*negotiate*" means within the Regulations. Cases on this point are now rare, but occasionally principals continue to try to avoid the Regulations on this basis.

In *Parks v Esso Petroleum,*[20] Mr Parks ran a petrol station and was paid commission on sales. Whilst the agreement described the petrol station operator as an agent, as a result of the lack of active involvement in the selling process, Mr Parks was held by the court not to be a commercial

---

18 In *Pluczenik Diamond Company NV v W Nagel (a firm)* [2018] EWCA Civ 2640 (Comm) a purchasing agent was held to be a commercial agent within the meaning of the Regulations

19 [1996] CLC 1952

20 [1999] 18 Tr LR 232

agent for the purposes of the Regulations. The Court of Appeal took a broad approach to the meaning of negotiate, and explained that in order to negotiate, an agent does not need to "*haggle*", but does need, to adopt the definition of negotiate from the Oxford English Dictionary, to "*deal with, manage or conduct*" the sale on behalf of the principal. Unsurprisingly, in the Esso case, the Court held "*the motorist would be astonished to be told when he inserted the nozzle of the pipe into the top of his petrol tank that he was "negotiating" with the site operator*" and as a result, Mr Parks did not benefit from the protections contained within the Regulations.

The question of the meaning of "*negotiate*" within the Regulations was revisited in *PJ Pipe and Valve Co Ltd v Audco India Ltd.*[21] In that case, the agent represented a manufacturer of valves used in the construction of petrochemical plants. The agent's role was to promote Audco's valves to a number of contractors. However, in circumstances where the court agreed that "*it is undoubtedly the case that PJV* [the agent] *did not have authority to negotiate sales in the sense that they were not empowered to agree terms or pricing*", the question was did the agent negotiate at all?

Referring to the fact that the purpose of the Regulations it to protect agents and to give them a stake in the goodwill they generate for their principals, and that as a result the courts should avoid a limited or restricted interpretation of the word "*negotiate*" that would exclude agents who have been engaged to develop the principal's business, the court held that the agent was a commercial agent and benefitted from the Regulations. The judge said:

> "*PJV's role* [i.e. the agent's role] w*as to deal with and conduct (and, in part, manage) the relevant discussions and transactions …; in particular, they effected the crucial introductions and they played a significant role in persuading the contractor to be interested in AIL's* [i.e. the principal's] *products… Thereafter, they assisted in ensuring that their client was placed on the approved list of vendors and received the invitations to tender, in part by putting in an appropriate bid; they assisted with quotations and queries; and they provided feedback and advised on how the quotation could be improved. In*

21 [2005] EWHC 1904 (QB)

> *both the short and the long term they were retained, inter alia, to develop goodwill on the part of AIL.... I conclude PJV acted as a commercial agent for the purposes of the Regulations, notwithstanding their lack of authority to progress agreement on commercial terms or prices."*

The courts have continued to construe "*negotiate*" widely. In a case relating to the sale of wine, the High Court Judge hearing the case said: "*I agree that the word "negotiate" (and its equivalents in other languages of the EU) is to be widely construed*".[22]

That said, some principals continue to argue the point. In *Green Deal Marketing Southern Ltd v Economy Energy Trading Ltd & Ors*[23], the principal (EE) argued that the field sales agent (GDM), which visited people at home and tried to get them to switch energy supplier, was not negotiating in the relevant sense.

The Judge disagreed and held that GDM was negotiating, within the meaning of the Regulations, despite it not being involved in any subsequent sale of electricity or gas. He said:

> "*[144] I accept that GDM had authority to, and did, negotiate the sale of goods on behalf of EE. It is correct, as Mr Green points out, that GDM did not directly negotiate sales of energy but rather acted in respect of signing the customers up to a switch of energy providers, who then made the sales themselves. However, the courts have construed the Regulations broadly so as to bring work such as that done by GDM within the scope of the definition.*"

"Goods" – but what about services?

Regulation 2 provides that agents who sell goods benefit from the protection of the Regulations. Implicitly, this excludes agents who sell services. This was also the position under the Directive. The reason for this is not immediately obvious and may have something to do with the fact that a principal who has to provide an ongoing service to a customer

---

22 *Invicta v International Brands Limited* [2013] EWHC 1564 (QB).

23 [2019] EWHC 507 (Ch)

builds (and is able to damage) his own goodwill and therefore, the agent does not generate and should not share in that goodwill.[24]

On the face of it, the difference between goods and services may seem obvious: for example, medical devices are goods, insurance is a service. If only it were that simple. For example, is gas or electricity a good? What about software?

The Regulations contain no definition of "*goods*" and the official guidance issued by the government at the time the Regulations came in to force is of little assistance. Therefore, it is not surprising that principals and agents have litigated upon whether a particular product is a good or a service. Fortunately, the courts have provided some clarity, though as will be seen, some uncertainties remain, particularly in relation to software.

The courts have held in *Tamarind International Ltd v Eastern Natural Gas (Retail) Ltd*[25] that gas is a good for the purposes of the Regulations, and in another case that electricity is too.[26]

The position in respect of software is still unresolved. In *St Albans City and District Council v International Computers Ltd* [1996] 4 ALL ER, the court held that a computer disk is within the definition of goods within the Sale of Goods Act 1979 and the Supply of Goods and Services Act 1982 but a computer program is not. In *Accentuate v Asigra Inc* [2009] EWHC 2655 (QB), the court stated that software is intellectual property and therefore not a good, whereas hardware is.

In *Computer Associates UK Ltd v Software Incubator Limited*[27], the Court of Appeal concluded that where software is supplied electronically and not on any tangible medium, it cannot be classified as "*goods*". As a result, agents who promote software which is supplied electronically, rather than

24 Note that as discussed below the Directive has been implemented in some member states (e.g France) so that it does apply to the sale of services.

25 [2000] CLC1397

26 *Green Deal Marketing Southern Ltd v Economy Energy Trading Ltd & Ors* [2019] EWHC 507 (Ch)

27 [2018] EWCA Civ 518

on a CD or USB drive, do not benefit from the protections provided by the Regulations.

That decision was appealed to the Supreme Court and at the time of writing the appeal is outstanding. The Supreme Court has now referred that question to the Court of Justice of the European Union. As a result, it will be some time before we have any clarity on this point.

In the case of *Pace Airline Services v Aerotrans Luftfahrtagentur GmBH* (unreported) it was suggested that cargo space on an aircraft could be goods. The issue was due to be resolved by the CJEU, but the case was settled before it got to that court.

However, in the case of *Crane v Sky In-home Services and others,*[28] Sky television digital packages (as distinct from the Sky+ boxes) were agreed by the parties to be services and not goods; and thus that the dominant purpose of the material contractual relationship was not the sale of goods but the sale of a service.

Generally, it will not be too difficult to decide whether the items sold by an agent are 'goods' so as to bring them within the protection of the Regulations. But what about agents that sell goods and services? Clearly, it is possible that an agent will be engaged to procure orders for a principal's goods, as well as for services subsequently provided by a principal (for example, consultancy services). Denying commercial agents that sell their principals' goods and services the benefit of the Regulations would appear to run contrary to the purpose of the Regulations. However, it has been suggested in *Saintier & Scholes, Commercial Agents and The Law, LLP, 2005,* that where the provision of goods is merely ancillary to the provision of services, the Regulations will not apply, and vice versa. In other words, depending on whether the sale of goods is primary or secondary, the Regulations will either apply or not apply, but in either case they will apply or not apply to the whole contract (goods and services). This view has much to commend it, and it is difficult to disagree with Lord Drummond Young in the Scottish case of *Lloyd Gailey v Environmental Waste Control,*[29] in which he said: "*it is the nature of the principal's business that*

28 [2007] EWHC 66 (ChD)

29 [2004] EULR 423

should determine whether agents' activities are primary or secondary. If that business is not predominantly one involving the sale of goods, I am of opinion that the agents' activities are necessarily secondary".

Clearly then, each case will turn on its own facts, as shown by *Marjandi v Bon Accord*,[30] in which it was held that an agent selling conservatories and their installation was not selling goods as the agent procured the sale of both materials (i.e. goods) and labour (i.e. services).

The fact that the English Regulations cover only goods could prove troublesome where the parties are not both operating within the UK, since in some EU countries, such as France, agents that sell and buy services as well as goods are deemed to be commercial agents. This clearly has implications for principals based in the UK who engage agents based in EU countries.

What about sub-agents?

In practice there are numerous arrangements where a principal engages a single agent to sell its goods in, for example, the UK. That agent then engages a number of agents itself in order to effectively cover the territory. This arrangement raises some tricky legal issues. For example:

1. If the managing agent simply manages, rather than seeks to sell products itself, is it a commercial agent at all?
2. If the managing agent is primarily managing agents and only selling as a secondary function, do the Regulations apply?
3. Are the sub-agents commercial agents within the meaning contained within the Regulations in circumstances where they have no contractual obligations or liabilities to the principal?

On the first and second issues, the managing agent clearly has continuing authority to negotiate the sale or purchase of goods on behalf of another person, which authority it derives from its contract with the principal; the fact that it exercises that authority through sub-agents is irrelevant to the question of authority. However, its managing duties may mean that

30 [2007] Scot SC 55

its activities as a commercial agent are secondary (an issue which is considered further later). That said, the Court of Appeal's view in a case involving a managing agent was that it could see no reason why that managing agent did not have a claim for compensation against the principal based on the management aspect of the work and the sub-agents' success in promoting and selling the principals' products.[31] This view was *obiter* (i.e. judicial comment) and so is not binding law and is liable to challenge as principals will have arguments that the court did not fully consider the issue when it came to this view. Further, the issue of secondary activities was not in dispute in that case.

The sub-agent's position is – under the current state of the law – less comfortable. In *Light and others v Ty Europe*,[32] the High Court Judge who heard the case held that sub-agents had authority to act on behalf of the principal and so benefited from the Regulations. Ty Europe appealed to the Court of Appeal and argued that in order for the Regulations to apply to the agency relationship, there had to be a contract between the principal and its agents.

The Court of Appeal agreed with Ty Europe's view that in order for the Regulations to apply to an agent, the agent must have a contract (which could be written or implied) with the principal. In the case of sub-agents, their contract is with the managing agent.

The court explained, rather colourfully, its view that:

> "*If any sub-agent selling goods on behalf of the manufacturer, importer or distributor was its commercial agent there would inevitably be chaos and confusion. How would the principal know who all his commercial agents were? Would sub-sub-agents also be included? … Might he be liable to pay commission or compensation both to the agent and the sub-agent? If the principal's relationship is governed by the contract which he has with his agent, supplemented as necessary by the Regulations, no such uncertainties arise.*"

31 *Light and others v Ty Europe* [2003] EWCA Civ 1238

32 [2003] EWCA Civ 1238

This decision has come in for some criticism from commentators. However, there is force in the argument that it is hardly appropriate for a principal to be liable to a sub-agent under the Regulations in circumstances where he has no contract with that agent and therefore no mechanism by which he can manage and deal with that agent. In any event, the law on this point is settled – unless a brave and deep-pocketed sub-agent wishes to challenge the Court of Appeal's judgment on this issue.

The issue of sub-agency also creates some very interesting arguments on the calculation of post-termination payments under Regulation 17, which are considered later.

Secondary activities

Agents whose activities as commercial agents "*are to be considered secondary*" are excluded from the Regulations.[33] The Schedule to the Regulations sets out how one should assess whether an agent's activities as a commercial agent are secondary. The difficulty for agents, principals and practitioners is that the Schedule is, to say the least, not the easiest to comprehend. Indeed, in one case, the Court of Appeal made very forthright comments about it.[34] Lord Justice Waller said he was "*quite bewildered*" by the Schedule, whilst Lord Justice Peter Gibson said with a large degree of understatement that the schedule was "*unhappily worded*".

This created difficulties for parties and their advisers for a time when considering whether an agent's activities as commercial agents are secondary. That said, the courts have grappled with the Schedule and have provided helpful guidance on its application.

First, what the Schedule is not concerned with is the quantitatively prevalent type of activity performed by the agent during the agency. The question is not how much time the agent devoted to commercial agency activities versus other activities. What it is concerned with is, as stated in the Schedule, *"the primary purpose"* of the agency contract and whether the principal's appointment of the agent was to *"devote effort, skill and*

33 Regulations 2(3) and 2(4).

34 *AMB Imballaggi Plastici SRL v Pacflex Limited* 1999 WL 477352

expenditure" to assist the principal *"in developing the market in the [material] goods"*.

Second, the time at which the primary purpose of the agency contract must be established is at the time that contract is made.

The proper approach to construing the Schedule is now fairly well-established, in particular by the Court of Appeal in *Michael Edwards v International Connection (UK) Ltd*[35] and Briggs J in *Crane v Sky In-Home Service Ltd & Anor*.[36]

In summary:

1. If there are equal "*primary purposes*" of the agency, then the Regulations apply: *Edwards*, per Moore-Bick LJ at 15; per Arden LJ at 25-28; *Crane* at 54.

2. The question of the primary purpose of the agency contract is to be determined by reference to paragraph 2 of the Schedule; the *"indications"* in paragraphs 3 and 4 are intended only to *"provide assistance in deciding whether the arrangement under consideration does or does not fall within paragraph 2 without being determinative of the question one way or the other"*: *Edwards*, per Moore-Bick LJ at 14 (also at 17); and *Crane* at 56-59.

3. In establishing what was the primary purpose of the agency contract pursuant to paragraph 2 of the Schedule, it is irrelevant what activities were actually performed (*a fortiori* as those may have changed over time). As Moore-Bick LJ stated at paragraph 19 of Edwards:

   > *"Paragraph 2 itself is not directly concerned with what is actually done pursuant to the arrangement, but with the characteristics of the arrangement itself and the reference in paragraph 2(b)(i) to transactions being 'normally individually negotiated and con-*

35 [2006] EWCA Civ 662

36 [2007] EWHC 66 (Ch)

cluded on a commercial basis' is not a reference to what has occurred pursuant to the arrangement but to the nature of the goods to which that arrangement relates".

The commodities exception

As noted above, the Court of Appeal has considered when a commercial agent may be operating on a commodity exchange or in the commodity market, a question which is important because the Regulations provide that they do not apply to "*commercial agents when they operate on commodity exchanges or in the commodity market*".[37]

In *Pluczenik Diamond Co NV v W Nagel (A Firm),*[38] the agent (Nagel) worked as the principal's (Pluczenik's) broker, assisting it to purchase diamonds from De Beers. The purchases were made at so-called "Sights", which were organised sales which could only be attended by purchasers accredited by De Beers as a "Sightholder".

In the High Court proceedings, the Judge found that purchases of diamonds made at Sights were made "*on commodity exchanges or in the commodity market*" and therefore the Regulations did not apply.[39]

On appeal, the Court of Appeal disagreed with the Judge's findings on the application of the commodities exception in this case and agreed with Nagel's case that the Regulations did apply.[40]

In doing so the Court of Appeal clarified the commodities exception in the Regulations and held that:

1. The relevant question is not whether the goods were sold as a commodity but whether they were sold on a "*commodity exchange*" or in "*the commodity market*".

37 Regulation 2(2)(b)

38 [2018] EWCA Civ 2640

39 Notwithstanding this, the majority of Nagel's claims succeeded and it was awarded very substantial damages for breach of contract, as well as commission on transactions which were not disclosed to it during the life of the contract.

40 The Court of Appeal also rejected Pluczenik's appeal against the damages awarded for breach of contract as being "*entirely without merit*"

2. An essential feature of a commodity exchange is that the commodities (or rights to buy and sell commodities) which are traded on the exchange can be freely bought and sold among the participants.

3. The commodity market encompasses any general trading in commodities that takes place in the open market.

The Court of Appeal concluded that the Sights would not be understood by commercial people as a commodity exchange nor would sales made by De Beers at such Sights be understood as trading in the commodity market. Whilst Pluczenik sought permission to appeal to the Supreme Court, its application was rejected and this Court of Appeal guidance will be of assistance to principals and agents in future.

Distributors and agents

In some other jurisdictions, distributors benefit from protections similar to the Regulations. However, as noted above, the Regulations do not apply to distributors.

In a notable decision on this point, *AMB Imballaggi Plastici SRL v Pacflex Ltd*,[41] Peter Gibson LJ said:

> "*The plain implication of the language of the directive and of the regulations is that if the sale or purchase of goods is negotiated by the intermediary in its own interest rather than on behalf of the principal, the intermediary is not a commercial agent. The paradigm example of an intermediary so negotiating is as a distributor purchasing goods from the manufacturer but reselling the goods for a profit on the mark-up.*"

That said, there may be situations where agents purchase and resell goods as well as act as commercial agents. The facts of such cases will need careful consideration by both agents and principals when it comes to assessing

41 *AMB Imballaggi Plastici SRL v Pacflex Ltd [1999]* 2 All ER (Comm) 249; also cited in *Mercantile International Group Plc v Chuan Soon Huat Industrial Group Ltd* [2002] EWCA Civ 288

whether the agent benefits from the Regulations; for example, the secondary activities exception may then be engaged, if both activities are performed pursuant to a single contract.

CHAPTER 3

APPLICABLE LAW AND JURISDICTION – THE TERRITORIAL APPLICATION OF THE REGULATIONS – PRACTICAL AND LEGAL GUIDE – Regulations 1(2) and 1(3)

It is very often the case that agency contracts are international contracts. For example, a US-based manufacturer may wish to sell its products in the UK through an agent, or an Italian textile mill may wish to use an agent to sell its fabric to English businesses.

The application of the Regulations, in such circumstances, can cause complexities to arise and can cause principals based outside the UK, and especially outside the EU, particular difficulties.

The starting point in respect of applicable law can be found in Regulations 1(2) and 1(3):

> "*(2) These Regulations govern the relations between commercial agents and their principals and, subject to paragraph (3), apply in relation to the activities of commercial agents in Great Britain.*
>
> "*(3) A court or tribunal shall:*
>
> *(a) apply the law of the other member State concerned in place of regulations 3 to 22 where the parties have agreed that the agency contract is to be governed by the law of that member State;*
>
> *(b) (whether or not it would otherwise be required to do so) apply these regulations where the law of another member State corresponding to these regulations enables the parties to agree that the agency contract is to be governed by the law of a different member State and the parties have agreed that it is to be governed by the law of England and Wales or Scotland.*"

Key points to note

1. The Regulations will apply where the agent conducts its activities in Great Britain, whether or not the parties have a written contract. Accordingly, and by way of illustration, an agent who lives in the south of France, but who conducts sales activities in Great Britain, would be likely to benefit from the Regulations.

2. If an agent undertakes its activities in a non-EEA country, and the contract specifies English law, then unless it is expressly agreed that the Regulations apply, they will not be applicable.

3. If the parties agree that the law of an EEA member state other than England is to apply to their contract, then that law will apply and the law implementing the Directive in that jurisdiction will apply (i.e. the Regulations will have no application).

4. If an agent in another EEA state and its principal agree that the Regulations (or more likely, English law), apply to their relationship, provided that state enables them to agree that a foreign law applies to their contract, the Regulations will apply.

5. If the parties' contract (where the agent's activities are conducted in Great Britain) contains an applicable law clause choosing non-EU law, or a jurisdiction clause choosing a forum which would result in proceedings in which the Regulations may or would not be applied, then the English court will apply the Regulations.[42]

It is this last point that arises most in practice when pursuing claims before the English courts for English-based agents who act for non-EU-based principals and whose contracts expressly choose the law of a non-EU state. The reason that the English court will apply the English Regulations in the face of an express choice of non-EU law is that the Regulations contain overriding mandatory provisions of EU law, which the English courts are obliged to apply. So if a contract between an agent conducting its activities in Great Britain, and a principal in, for example, California, contains an applicable law clause in favour of Californian state

42 Note however that, as considered below, the position is less clear after the UK exits the EU on 31 December 2020.

law, the agent could bring claims under the Regulations in the English court.

In *Ingmar v Eaton Leonard Technologies Ltd,*[43] the agent was based in the UK and the principal was based in California, USA. The contract between the parties included a choice of law clause in favour of Californian law. The High Court ruled that the Regulations did not apply and the agent appealed to the Court of Appeal. The Court of Appeal referred the following question of the applicability of the Regulations to the European Court of Justice (the "**ECJ**", as the Court of Justice of the European Union was then named):

> "*Whether Articles 17 and 18 of the Directive* [which are mirrored in Regulations 17 and 18 of the Regulations], *which guarantee certain rights to commercial agents after termination of agency contracts, must be applied where the commercial agent carried on his activity in a Member State although the principal is established in a non-member country and a clause of the contract stipulates that the contract is governed by the law of that country*" (paragraph 14).

The ECJ answered the question as follows:

> "[25] *It must therefore be held that it is essential for the Community legal order that a principal established in a non-Member country, whose commercial agent carries on his activity within the Community, cannot evade those provisions by the simple expedient of a choice-of-law clause. The purpose served by the provisions in question requires that they be applied where the situation is closely connected with the Community, in particular where the commercial agent carries on his activity in the territory of a Member State, irrespective of the law by which the parties intended the contract to be governed.*
>
> "[26] *In the light of those considerations, the answer to the question must be that Articles 17 and 18 of the Directive, which guarantee certain rights to commercial agents after termination of agency contracts, must be applied where the commercial agent carried on his activity in a Member State although the principal is established in a*

43 [2001] CMLR 9 ECJ

> *non-Member country and a clause of the contract stipulates that the contract is to be governed by the law of that country*".

In *United Antwerp Maritime Agencies (Unamar) NV v Navigation Maritime Bulgare,*[44] the ECJ said:

> "*Articles 17 and 18 of the Directive are of crucial importance*" and "*the regime established by Directive 86/653 for that purpose* [i.e. giving commercial agents protection via Articles 17 and 18 of the Directive] *is mandatory in nature*".

The judgment of the ECJ in *Ingmar* was followed by the High Court in *Accentuate Ltd v Asigra Inc,*[45] in which Tugendhat J stated:

> "[79] *For all present purposes this Court acts as a Community Court and is obliged to give effect to the Claimant's mandatory Regulation 17 rights*";
>
> "[88] *The decision in Ingmar requires this Court to give effect to the mandatory provisions of EU law, notwithstanding any expression to the contrary on the part of the contracting parties.*"

As a result, in *Accentuate*, Tugendhat J concluded (at paragraph 93) that the claimant's claim could be served out of the jurisdiction as its claim for compensation under the Regulations was a claim made in respect of a contract where the contract was governed by English law, notwithstanding that the contract in that case was expressly governed by the law of Ontario.

So far, so clear. However, in *Fern Computer Consultancy Ltd v Intergraph Cadworx & Analysis Solutions Inc,*[46] Mr Justice Mann disagreed with Tugendhat J's view in *Accentuate* that in circumstances where a contract of commercial agency between an English agent and a US principal was expressly governed by the law of a US state, that contract could be said to be governed by English law.

---

44 (C-184/12)

45 [2009] EWHC 2655 (QB)

46 [2014] EWHC 2908 (Ch)

Mr Justice Mann did however find that the claim under the Regulations would be governed by English law (at paragraph 40 he said the claim was "*undoubtedly governed by English law*") and suggested, as a solution to the problem potentially created for agents by his analysis, that the claim would be for breach of statutory duty with the damage sustained within the jurisdiction – an approach that would entitle the agent to bring its claim in England.

Once the UK has left the EU, however, the position may be different. The courts of the UK will no longer be *"Community Courts"* and the 'mandatory' force of the Directive will no longer apply in the UK. Whilst the UK courts (except the Supreme Court and Court of Appeal) remain bound by EU case law decided before 1 January 2021, the ratio of *Ingmar* – that the Directive (and in particular, Article 17) must be applied across the EU because the material provisions are mandatory rules in each EU state – is likely to be inapplicable as the UK will not be an EU member state. It may then be possible for parties to a contract which is to be performed in Great Britain to agree that the contract will be governed by the law of a non-EU state; and if they do so, that choice may be effective in excluding the Regulations. That said, it remains to be seen if the courts will take the UK's departure from the EU as an opportunity to remove the protections that had hitherto been afforded to commercial agents in such a scenario, and some agents are likely to continue to pursue claims in England under the Regulations until the position is definitively clarified. The precise wording of any law and jurisdiction clause is likely to be important.

Activities in multiple jurisdictions

What happens when the agent carries out their activities in multiple jurisdictions? It is not uncommon for an agent to act on behalf of its principal in more than one state and therefore, the question for an agent who acts in both Great Britain and elsewhere is: do the Regulations apply?

In *Wood Floor Solutions Andreas Domberger GmbH v Silva Trade SA,*[47] the ECJ concluded that where, under a contract, services were provided in several member states, the court within the jurisdiction of which the

47 (Case C-19/09)

place of the main provision of services was situated was the one which had jurisdiction to hear and determine all the claims arising from the contract. The court held that, for a commercial agency contract, that place was the place of the main provision of services by the agent, as it appeared from the provisions of the contract or, in the absence of such provisions, the actual performance of that contract or, where it could not be established on that basis, the place where the agent was domiciled.

CHAPTER 4A

RIGHTS AND OBLIGATIONS OF AGENT AND PRINCIPAL DURING THE AGENCY – PRACTICAL GUIDE

Practical guide to what the Regulations require of agent and principal during the agency: money (commission); cooperation; issues of competition (other agencies, etc.).

Good faith and cooperation

Both agent and principal have to act 'dutifully and in good faith' towards each other. Leaving aside for the moment the issue of an agent acting for 'competing' principals, the Regulations give what they consider the main components of that duty on each side:-

Agent- to make proper efforts to win the business; to give all necessary information to the principal; to comply with reasonable instructions.

Principal – to provide all necessary documents and information and tell the agent promptly if it is not going to accept any relevant order(s).

What do these duties mean in practice, and what is the consequence if they are not adhered to?

The agent, for instance, may not agree with the principal about what constitutes 'proper efforts', or 'necessary information'. Principals and agents frequently fall out because the principal wants the agent to put more time and effort into that agency than the agent considers necessary or obliged of him/her; or because the principal wants reports of every customer visit, say, but the agent considers that an unfairly onerous obligation (not a 'reasonable instruction'). And a lot more often than not, the written agency contract is rather vague on these points (if there is one at all).

As we saw earlier, it is of the essence of being a commercial agent that s/he/it is 'self-employed' and thus has a certain degree of autonomy. If a principal attempts in effect to turn the agent into an employee, the agent is entitled to resist. Still less will the failure of an agent to perform according to the expectations of their principal in terms of the number of sales achieved (probably the commonest reason for termination of an agency) amount to a breach of the agent's duties under the Regulations.

However, being self-employed is not a charter for obstinacy or lack of cooperation. If a principal introduces a new system of order-management and asks its agents to use it, an agent who refuses because s/he prefers the old system will very likely be in breach of her/his obligations. The same will apply if a principal makes modest requests for reports on customer visits (monthly or quarterly perhaps).

On the other side of the coin, an agent may want certain support from his/her principal, which the principal is unwilling to provide. A request to be copied in to every piece of email correspondence with customers is likely to be an unreasonable one; an expectation that the principal will tell the agent of any significant meeting with a customer serviced by the agent would probably be regarded as sensible.

It is difficult to be too prescriptive in the abstract – what might be reasonable for one agent or principal to demand, might be inappropriate for another. A principal who delays in providing samples by a couple of weeks to an agent working in women's fashions will be much more likely to have breached its obligations than a principal whose business is the sale of nuts and bolts.

Tip for agents and principals: If the other party makes a request for something that is not covered by the agency contract, you may still be obliged to cooperate if the request is a clearly reasonable one.

Consequences of breach

As with any breach of a contractual or statutory obligation, there are several possible consequences:-

(1) The breach(es) could be relatively minor and have no direct financial consequence. In that case the party affected can do little other than reg-

ister concern. If those breaches continue, or if other similar breaches happen in the following weeks, there may come a point where, looking at all of those minor breaches together, they 'add up' to a serious breach.

An agent, for instance, who consistently fails to produce quarterly reports or misses half of the monthly sales meetings is in much more danger of having committed a serious breach of his/her duties under the Regulations than one whose lapse was on only one occasion.

(2) The breach could be relatively minor, but have a direct financial consequence. In that case, the affected party can demand to be compensated for its loss.

A principal, for instance, who negligently fails to provide a sample requested by the agent on behalf a customer who as a result has to source the product it wanted elsewhere on that occasion, is liable to pay its agent the commission s/he would have earned on the sale (assuming it can be shown that had the sample been provided, the sale would have been won).

An agent who without excuse fails to return a customer's urgent call, as the result of which a sale is lost, is – at least in theory – liable to pay the principal the lost net profit it would have made on that sale.

(3) The breach could be serious. In that case, the party affected has the *right* to terminate the agency contract without penalty (and in the principal's case, without paying compensation or indemnity: see below), provided they do so reasonably promptly. That party is *not obliged* to terminate the agency contract; and if they do not, they may still demand to be compensated for any financial loss.

Again, what constitutes a serious breach may vary from agency to agency. Some matters are clear-cut: a principal who refuses to pay commissions owed; an agent who goes around telling customers that his principal's products are of poor quality – these actions will always constitute serious breaches. However, the seriousness of the breach of an agent who misses without good cause a training meeting organised by his/her principal, might vary depending on whether the products are furniture, say, or a brand new range of sophisticated electronic equipment about to be launched at a trade show in the agent's territory.

Competing products

As a self-employed person, an agent is generally free to – and often does – represent several principals whose ranges do not compete/conflict. However, this can often become a thorny issue, with the agent believing that no conflict exists between the range of one principal and another, but with one (or both) principal(s) disagreeing.

Competing and conflicting ranges

An example: Two companies both make women's clothes.

(1) It may be that the two ranges are obviously non-competitive – one may be bridal wear, the other swimsuits; or they may both be bridal wear, but one range sells into high street stores for £250 per item, the other range only into exclusive fashion shops at £3,000 per item. In these situations the ranges neither compete nor conflict.

(2) Perhaps both companies make dresses, at roughly the same price point and aimed at the same age-group; but one is made from artificial fabrics and is dyed in bright colours; the other is made from white cotton. Assume that it is most unlikely that an end customer would be choosing between the two ranges in a shop. It could well be said that the two ranges are not conflicting, they do not 'overlap' – but might they compete? If they are being promoted to the same shops with limited budgets and shelf-space, it might well be the case that the more of one range that the agent sells, the less of the other s/he is likely to be able to sell. That said, the shop might prefer a selection of white and bright-coloured dresses. In that situation, whether the agent acts in breach of duty is at best unclear.

(3) Of course, if the ranges actually overlap to any meaningful extent – both ranges include cotton dresses at similar prices aimed at similar ages/types of women – then they will conflict in the classic sense. For an agent to promote both would be a serious dereliction of duty, save in the unlikely event that both principals had expressly consented to that happening, knowing what they were agreeing to.

Transparency

The easiest and best way of avoiding this issue causing problems is for the parties – the agent in particular – to make sure that the position is transparent. The prudent agent makes sure when commencing an agency that his/her new principal is told, in writing, of the other principals s/he acts for, and does the same in respect of any further principals whose agencies s/he takes on thereafter.

So long as the principal has been told and given all relevant details, or at least offered the chance to request them, and does not object, it will be very difficult for it to object subsequently.

Tip for agent: Make sure you have told your principal, in writing, of your other agencies, particularly any new agency you take on which might possibly be thought to compete, even if you do not believe it does.

Changing product ranges

It sometimes happens that an agent represents two principals whose product ranges do not compete, but that one principal then extends its range so that now the two ranges do compete. Provided that is not done for an ulterior motive (to put the agent in an impossible situation), that might lead to a genuine commercial difficulty which it is the agent's responsibility to tackle.

If the agent is permitted not to carry the extensions to the range, all will be well. However, that may not be commercially practical. If it is not, and if one or both of the principals concerned will not tolerate the potential conflict, then the agent is put in the invidious position of having to choose between the agencies – but choose s/he must.

Tip for principal: If you want to extent your product range, check with your agents whether that might cause any potential conflict with ranges they carry for other principals.

Tip for agent: If your principal extends its product range, make sure you raise with it any potential conflict with ranges you carry for other principals; and raise it also with those other principals.

Commissions

The first and main issue which tends to arise between parties in relation to commission is: on which sales is the agent entitled to be paid commission?

First, the agent is entitled to commission on any sales which fall within those categories identified within the agency contract (if there is one). Beyond that, the situation becomes more interesting.

The Regulations (Reg. 7) provide for three situations where commission must be paid:

(1) The first is rarely if ever controversial: where the order has been won by the actions of the agent.

(2) The second is also generally not controversial: where the agency contract (even if only oral) grants the agent an *exclusive* group or area of customers, then sales to those customers entitle the agent to commission. After all, there is otherwise no meaning to exclusivity.

(3) The third situation is more controversial: where the agent won the customer for the principal some time previously, but has had no involvement in certain subsequent sales under consideration (and does not have exclusivity). Principals often feel entitled in such situations to cease paying commission to the agent – perhaps to 'turn the account into a house account'. If the contract is silent on the point, then the Regulations serve to *protect* the agent's right to commissions in those circumstances, where otherwise the right would probably not exist.

See the next chapter for what happens if a principal seeks to impose such a change to the agency terms on an unwilling agent.

What if the contract and the Regulations clash?

What if, in the last situation, there was an agency contract which stated that unless the agent was directly involved in obtaining an order s/he would not be entitled to commission on it? Would the agent be entitled to rely on the Regulations anyway?

Surprisingly, there is no clear answer to this yet – and experts in the field take different views.

Legal advice warning: If this issue arises, it is probably best to seek legal advice.

Can two agents have a right to commission on the same transaction?

It is sometimes the case, for instance, that an agent sells to a customer on another agent's exclusive territory, or that an order is placed with a customer's buyer in one territory for delivery to stores in other territories.

It may be that the agency contract – or long custom and practice – will have addressed these situations. If not, then problems can arise.

In the situation where an agent sells to a customer in a second agent's exclusive territory, it would seem that the second agent is definitely entitled to commission. The first agent, if s/he has not acted in breach of contract, may also be entitled to commission.

In the situation where the customer's head office is not in the same territory as those in which the stores are situated where the goods are delivered, it would normally be the case that the agents in those other territories would not be entitled to commission; but if the orders were in effect won in the individual territories and simply placed through the customer's head office, then the situation might be reversed.

Tip for principal: Try to ensure that your agency contracts cover the situation where a customer's buyer or head office is based in one territory, but retail outlets are based in others (if that might happen).

At what point in time does commission become 'due' and payable?

This is not often a cause for dispute (as opposed to the principal simply not paying at the agreed times).

The Regulations provide in effect that:

(1) In the absence of any contractual agreement to the contrary, commission becomes 'due' when the goods are delivered, or on the due date for delivery, or the customer pays, whichever happens first.

(2) Whatever the contract says, commission in any event becomes 'due' at the latest when the customer pays, or was due to pay assuming the principal delivered on time.

(3) Once commission is 'due', then it must be paid no later than the end of the month following the quarter in which it became due – successive quarters beginning on the dates the agency began, 3 months, 6 months and 9 months afterwards. This last provision is rarely relied on because the agency contract (or at least custom and practice) will normally have provided for a less complicated method of establishing the date commission payments should be made – and one generally more favourable to the agent.

What if the order is cancelled?

The Regulations provide that the agent remains entitled to commission if the order is cancelled, by either the principal or the customer, *unless the reason for cancellation is one for which the principal was not to blame.*

Thus if the principal does not fulfil the order, or delivers so late that the customer refuses the goods, the agent must still be paid commission.

If, however, the customer refuses to take delivery on time, or simply does not pay the principal – or if the transaction is not completed through no fault of either principal or customer (the proverbial 'act of God') – then no commission is payable; indeed any commission paid can be set off or refunded.

Tip for agents and principals: If a principal cancels or fails to deliver an order, commission is very likely still due to the agent.

Commission statements, checking the books

The Regulations require principals to supply agents with commission statements at the time payment is due, showing how the total is calculated. It is not clear whether this requires the individual sales to be listed, though one would have thought so.

In any event, the principal is required to provide to an agent, on request, extracts from its 'books' (sales ledgers, etc.), sufficient to enable the agent to check the amount of commission properly due.

CHAPTER 4B

RIGHTS AND OBLIGATIONS OF AGENT AND PRINCIPAL DURING THE AGENCY – LEGAL GUIDE

Regulations 3, 4, 5, 6, 7, 9, 10, 11 and 12

Good faith and cooperation – agent and principal

The Regulations codify the fiduciary obligations that generally fall on agents at common law. But in what was a new development for common lawyers in England, they also imposed good faith obligations on principals.[48]

These obligations are set out in Regulations 3 and 4 and, because of Regulation 5, the parties cannot contract out of them.

Agent's duties

An agent's duties to his principal are set out in Regulation 3:

> *"3.— Duties of a commercial agent to his principal*
>
> *(1) In performing his activities a commercial agent must look after the interests of his principal and act dutifully and in good faith.*
>
> *(2) In particular, a commercial agent must—*
>
> *(a) make proper efforts to negotiate and, where appropriate, conclude the transactions he is instructed to take care of;*
>
> *(b) communicate to his principal all the necessary information available to him;*

48 Though note that the English courts will, in certain circumstances, imply the term of good faith into commercial contracts, such as in *Yam Seng Pte Ltd v International Trade Corp Ltd* [2013] EWHC 111; and that they imply a mutual duty of trust and confidence into all contracts of employment: see below under Principal's duties.

(c) comply with reasonable instructions given by his principal."

These obligations are not particularly onerous and are usually supplemented with further duties in a contract (and are overlaid by an agent's common-law duties as a fiduciary of his principal). Moreover, they are not new; an agent will be and has historically been subject to these obligations at common law.

But what happens if an agent breaches Regulation 3? Does that entitle the principal to terminate the contract and avoid paying compensation under Regulation 18(a)?

Legal status of Regulation 3

The issue of whether a breach of Regulation 3 would automatically entitle the principal to terminate the contract and avoid the operation of Regulation 17 was considered by the Court of Appeal in *Crocs Europe BV v Anderson (t/a Spectrum Agencies (A Partnership))*.[49]

In that case, some of the agent's employees had posted material on a website which the agent said was "a joke", but which the principal said was highly derogatory of it. A link to that website had been sent to other employees of the agent and to third parties, including some customers of the principal in the UK and distributors in other markets. The principal terminated the contract and argued that the agent had breached Regulation 3 and it had therefore been entitled to terminate and avoid paying a post-termination payment under Regulation 17, by virtue of Regulation 18(a).

The agent brought a claim against the principal under the Regulations and succeeded in the High Court. The principal appealed to the Court of Appeal, where it was argued by the principal that the good faith duty in Regulation 3 implies a condition into the agency contract and that a breach of that condition is always repudiatory.

The principal also argued that any breach of the fiduciary duty of loyalty owed by the agent to the principal necessarily and automatically results

49 [2012] EWCA Civ 1400

in the repudiation of the agency contract, such that the principal is entitled to terminate and avoid liability.

The Court of Appeal rejected both arguments, calling them "*far-fetched*". In respect of the implied condition argument, the Court said:

> "*There are insuperable difficulties in the defendant's argument on implied condition... Regulation 3 it is not expressed as, or to be, or to create a condition of the contract the breach of which will automatically terminate the agency contract. Regulation 3 does no more than set out the relevant obligations of the agent. There is no basis for holding that it goes further and implies them as fundamental conditions into the agency contract so that breach of them would always be repudiatory.*"

The Court of Appeal said that the argument that any breach of the fiduciary duty of loyalty necessarily and automatically results in the repudiation of the agency contract was a "*radical proposition*".

The court said that:

> "*fiduciary duties are not formulated in terms that produce the same outcome in the case of every breach. Breaches of fiduciary duty are capable of producing other consequences and remedial outcomes than simple termination of the fiduciary relationship. The remedial consequences of the breaches of duty depend not only on the nature of the duty owed but also on the factual circumstances in which the particular breach occurred and the intentions of the parties, as expressed or inferred, in relation to the contract. It would be an odd principle that separated the consequences of and available remedies for the breach from the surrounding circumstances of the particular case.*"

The court concluded that the question to be addressed was: "*how serious, in all the circumstances, was the claimant's conduct?*" Only if the breach went to the root of the contract would the principal be entitled to terminate based upon it without liability. In *Crocs*, the Judge in the High Court had been entitled to conclude, on the evidence before him, that the breach was not repudiatory.

Competing principals

Regulation 3 serves to underscore the common law on whether an agent can act for competing principals; an issue which was clarified in the context of commercial agency in the case of *Rossetti Marketing Ltd v Diamond Sofa Co Ltd.*[50]

In that case, the agent brought a claim against the principal under regulations 7, 8, 15 and 17 of the Regulations. The principal sought to defend the claim by contending, *inter alia*, that although it was unaware of its right (or the relevant facts giving rise to the right) at the time it terminated the agency arrangement with the agent, it had in fact had the right to put an end to the arrangement on the ground of the agent's breach of duty.[51] The breach of duty relied on was that the agent allegedly acted for two direct competitors of the principal.

The Court of Appeal re-affirmed that an agent owes a duty of loyalty to its principal, saying:

> "*As a general proposition, an agent occupies a fiduciary position vis-à-vis his principal. He owes what Millett LJ called 'the single-minded duty of loyalty' to his principal, so that he 'must not place himself in a position where his duty and his interest conflict', and he 'may not act for … the benefit of a third party without the informed consent of his principal' – Bristol and West Building Society v Mothew [1998] Ch 1, 18A-B. To the same effect, and more specifically to the present case, Lord Browne-Wilkinson, giving the judgment of the Privy Council in Kelly v Cooper [1993] AC 205, 214D, said that 'it is normally said that it is a breach of an agent's duty to act for competing principals'.*"

The Court of Appeal went on to state that an agent (who is not an estate agent) may only act for competing principals where both principals agree.[52] The Court said:

---

50 [2012] EWCA Civ 1021

51 The issue of the basis for a principal's termination, the reasons and the principal's knowledge are considered in below.

52 Estate agents are a special breed of agents to whom the non-compete principle does not apply, as they necessarily have many principals (sellers and buyers).

> "*In such a case, it is for the agent to show that the principal not merely consented, but that the consent was given on a fully informed basis – i.e. that the agent had made full disclosure to the principal.*"

In order not to be in breach of his duty of loyalty (and good faith), an agent who wishes to act for competing principals needs both of its principals' fully informed consent. It is suggested that this means that the principal is entitled to know what products the agent intends to sell for a competing principal and the identity of the customers to whom they are to be marketed. In circumstances where products are in direct competition, a principal's consent is unlikely to be forthcoming and indeed, provision of information by the agent to a competing principal, which might (if not in the public domain, such as in an online catalogue) be commercially sensitive, could itself be a serious breach of duty. An agent would be well advised to tread very cautiously in this respect.

What sorts of breaches of Regulation 3 have principals alleged?

In *Smith v Reliance Water Controls Limited,*[53] having failed to convince the court that the agent was an employee rather than an agent, the principal argued that the agent acted in breach of his duties to act dutifully and in good faith and that such failure disentitled him to compensation under the Regulations.

The principal argued that the agent failed to provide two specific items of information. The court was unimpressed and held:

> "[Counsel] *addressed us on the width of the duty of good faith. It is however, unnecessary to deal with his arguments in respect of this because, even accepting his submission in full and taking the duty at its widest, the facts of this case do not in my judgment come anywhere near falling within it… The principal's contention of lack of good faith does not reach first base.*"

In *Michael Edwards v International Connection (UK) Limited* (unreported), the issue was whether in the year and a half prior to termination, the agents' approach to his agency was fundamentally at odds with his

53 [2003] EuLR 874

obligation of good faith owed at common law and under the terms of regulation 3(a).

The argument advanced by the principal was that the evidence of customer feedback and sales generated showed that the agent was not making any proper effort to negotiate transactions. The Judge disagreed and said:

> "*I am unable to accept* [the principal's] *case that* [the agent's] *conduct and performance was repudiatory. While I accept that* [principal] *may have been disappointed with* [agent's] *sales, which fell below his expectation, in my judgment, the evidence comes nowhere* [sic – near] *supporting a claim of repudiatory breach, or indeed any breach by Mr. Edwards. I find that Mr. Edwards was not in repudiatory breach of his agency agreement and his agency was terminated in circumstances entitling him to compensation*".

In *Cureton v Mark Insulations Limited,*[54] the court concluded that the agent was in repudiatory breach of the agency agreement and Regulation 3 because it had sought, when acting for the principal, to make sales on behalf of a business that was owned and operated by the agent. Whilst the agent's business did not compete with the principal's, the court held that the agent was under a duty to disclose circumstances where its interests conflicted with that of the principal. As the principal was not made aware of the agent's business, the agent was in breach of its common law duties and the Regulation 3 good faith duty and the court found it a breach that was sufficient to justify termination.

In *Crane v Sky-in-Home Service Limited and Others,*[55] Sky-in-Home Service Limited ("SHS") alleged passing off by Mr Crane, on the basis that this amounted to a breach of his implied duty to look after the interests of his principal and to act dutifully and in good faith. In his judgment in

54 [2006] EWHC 2279

55 [2007] EWHC 66 (Ch)

the passing off claim,[56] Mr Justice Briggs found "*that Mr Crane was indeed the deliberate perpetrator of just such a persistent course of passing off*".[57] He also concluded that:

> "*Mr Crane was by February 2005 still deliberately and persistently passing off his extended warranty service as that of the Sky Group. That was a continuing and serious breach of his duty of fidelity to SHS. The person responsible for termination of* [the contract] *on behalf of SHS correctly believed that Mr Crane had continued in that course of conduct, and terminated* [the contract] *because of it.*"[58]

As a result, SHS could rely on Regulation 18(a) to avoid paying compensation.

The conclusion was the same in *Fryer v Ian Firth Hardware Limited,*[59] where the agent had been spending up to 30% of his time working on other things, despite a contractual obligation to *"work exclusively"* for the principal, and refusing to provide weekly reports.

Principal's duties

A principal's duties to his agent are set out in Regulation 4:

> "*4.— **Duties of a principal to his commercial agent***
>
> *(1) In his relations with his commercial agent a principal must act dutifully and in good faith.*
>
> *(2) In particular, a principal must—*
>
> *(a) provide his commercial agent with the necessary documentation relating to the goods concerned;*

56 [2006] EWHC 3165 (Ch)

57 [2007] EWHC 66 (Ch) at [86]

58 Ibid at [91]

59 [2008] EWHC 767(Ch)

(b) obtain for his commercial agent the information necessary for the performance of the agency contract, and in particular notify his commercial agent within a reasonable period once he anticipates that the volume of commercial transactions will be significantly lower than that which the commercial agent could normally have expected.

(3) A principal shall, in addition, inform his commercial agent within a reasonable period of his acceptance or refusal of, and of any non-execution by him of, a commercial transaction which the commercial agent has procured for him."

On its introduction this was entirely new; before the Regulations, a principal had very few obligations vis-à-vis his agent.

Regulations 4(2) and 4(3) are relatively straightforward. But what will constitute a breach of the obligation to act dutifully and in good faith? Potential arguments include where a principal tries to build relationships with customers procured by the agent behind the agent's back, or where the principal uses its superior negotiating power to impose a variation to the terms of the contract it has with the agent. The agent's claim in such circumstances will be in damages. In any event, in circumstances where the principal commits the breaches cited above, the agent may have a case under Regulation 18(b)(i); that is, the agent may be able to bring the contract to an end and claim compensation based on the principal's repudiation of the agreement.

The Court has considered Regulation 4 in a number of cases.

In *Vick v Vogle-Gapes Limited*[60] the court accepted that the principal's obligation to act towards its agent dutifully and in good faith was at least as wide as the obligation implied on the part an employer (and employee) in a contract of employment to act towards the other party with trust and confidence. The content of that obligation was formulated by the House of Lords in *Malik v. Bank of Credit and Commerce International SA* [1997] ICR 606, as being the relevant party (in that case the employer): *"shall not, without reasonable and proper cause, conduct itself in a manner*

60 [2006] EWHC 1579 (QB)

calculated [or] likely to destroy or seriously damage the relationship of confidence and trust between employer and employee." In *Vick*, the court held that the actions of the principal in unilaterally reducing the territory and market covered by the agency contract, pursuant to a term in that contract, had been done reasonably and with proper cause given the agent's prior poor conduct.

In *Simpson v Grant & Bowman Limited*,[61] the court held that:

1. A principal's duty to act in good faith towards its agent required a balance to be struck between the needs of the agent and the business needs of the principal. It did not require that all agents of a principal be treated the same.

2. In order to prove a breach of that duty, it was not necessary to show malice or bad faith on the part of the principal.

3. A breach of the duty would not automatically amount to a repudiatory breach of the agency contract unless it was sufficiently serious.

In *Cooper v Pure Fishing Limited*,[62] the agent acted for another principal in the same market, with both principals' consent, on the basis that there was no real conflict. However, after the passage of some time, the defendant principal decided to introduce a range of products that would conflict with the products of the agent's other principal. The agent objected and the principal alleged that the claimants' refusal to sell the new products amounted to a fundamental breach entitling it to terminate their contract and not pay compensation. As a result the principal allowed the contract to expire and did not offer the agent a new contract. When the agent claimed under the Regulations, the principal argued that: (a) there was no termination (as the contract expired) and therefore no entitlement to compensation; and (b) it had been entitled to terminate in any event as a result of the agent's breach in refusing to sell the new products.

The court found in the agent's favour and held that:

61 [2005] 8 WLUK 353

62 [2004] 2 Lloyds Rep 514

1. An agency contract is terminated for the purposes of the Regulations when it expires by effluxion of time and therefore the claims for compensation were not excluded by Regulation 18(a); and

2. The principal breached its duty of good faith by attempting to use its contractual rights to create a conflict of interest for the agent and had engineered the situation which it believed they would find intolerable in order to replace them with direct employees.

The Court of Appeal upheld the decision that expiry of the contract was a 'termination', but held that a principal could not rely on allowing the expiry of an agency contract as terminating the agency contract because of default attributable to the commercial agent which would justify immediate termination of the agency. Thus the agent was entitled to compensation and the Court of Appeal did not consider the judge's conclusion that in any event immediate termination of the agency contracts was not justified.

In *Npower Direct Ltd v South of Scotland Power Limited,*[63] the agent alleged that the principal had breached its duty of good faith by increasing the sales price of electricity, which led to a reduction in sales. The court held that the principal was not in breach on this basis as it had not increased prices in a manner which had made it impossible for the agent to make any, or any significant sales, and its prices were competitive.

Entitlement to commission[64] – when does it arise?

(a) Where there is no agreement as to commission

If the agent and principal have not agreed commission, or other remuneration, such as a retainer, recourse will be had to Regulation 6, which provides:

---

63 [2005] EWHC 2123 (Comm)

64 "Commission" is defined in Regulation 2(1) as: "*any part of the remuneration of a commercial agent which varies with the number or value of business transactions*".

"6.— Form and amount of remuneration in absence of agreement

(1) In the absence of any agreement as to remuneration between the parties, a commercial agent shall be entitled to the remuneration that commercial agents appointed for the goods forming the subject of his agency contract are customarily allowed in the place where he carries on his activities and, if there is no such customary practice, a commercial agent shall be entitled to reasonable remuneration taking into account all the aspects of the transaction.

(2) This regulation is without prejudice to the application of any enactment or rule of law concerning the level of remuneration.

(3) Where a commercial agent is not remunerated (wholly or in part) by commission, regulations 7 to 12 below shall not apply."

How Regulation 6(1) actually might operate in practice is potentially problematic; the Regulations do not provide a mechanism for determining what an agent in the particular field in question would customarily be paid, or what is "*reasonable remuneration taking into account all the aspects of the transaction*". Whilst the parties are likely to know what the going rate is in their particular field, this is clearly an area where disputes could arise; although it would be very unusual for a principal and an agent not to agree commission levels at the outset.

This issue arose in *PJ Pipe & Valve v Audco India*,[65] where conflicting evidence was given about the standard commissions in the oil, gas and petrochemical supply business and it was left to the Judge to decide the commissions payable.

It is noteworthy that the parties can exclude the entitlement to commission; that is, they can agree a different form of remuneration. In such a case, Regulations 7 to 12 will not apply.

---

65 [2005] EWHC 1904 (QB), paras 15 to 17 and 104 to 112

(b) Commissions on transactions concluded during agency contract

Regulation 7 fleshes out the circumstances in which the entitlement to commission arises during the term of the agency contract. It provides:

> "*7.— **Entitlement to commission on transactions concluded during agency contract***
>
> *(1) A commercial agent shall be entitled to commission on commercial transactions concluded during the period covered by the agency contract—*
>
> *(a) where the transaction has been concluded as a result of his action; or*
>
> *(b) where the transaction is concluded with a third party whom he has previously acquired as a customer for transactions of the same kind.*
>
> *(2) A commercial agent shall also be entitled to commission on transactions concluded during the period covered by the agency contract where he has an exclusive right to a specific geographical area or to a specific group of customers and where the transaction has been entered into with a customer belonging to that area or group.*"

Regulation 7(1)(a) provides that the commission is payable where the sale has been made by the principal as a result of the agent's action. Respected commentators contend that the "*as a result of*" formulation is a parallel of the common law "*effective cause*" rule.[66] Whether the agent is an effective cause of a transaction is an area for debate and there is a wealth of case law (outside the commercial agency sphere) on this issue.

Regulation 7(1)(b) entitles an agent to commissions on repeat orders. This would apply even if, after the initial order, the agent has no ongoing involvement. As explained in *Invicta v International Brands*[67]:

66 Bowstead & Reynolds on Agency, 20th Edn, para 11-029.

67 [2013] EWHC 1564 (QB)

> *"the activities of a commercial agent extend to procuring transactions and acquiring customers for repeat orders"*.

Regulation 7(2) protects an agent who has an exclusive right to a territory or a defined group of customers, in that if the principal receives orders from customers within that territory or customer group, the agent is entitled to commissions, even if the transaction has not resulted from the agent's actions (e.g. a direct approach from the customer to the principal).

(c) Commissions on transactions post-termination

Regulation 8 deals with an agent's entitlement to commission on transactions concluded after agency contract has terminated.

This is discussed in the Chapter "*Payments following termination*".

(d) Overlapping entitlements to commission between new and former agents

Regulation 9 provides:

> ***"9.— Apportionment of commission between new and previous commercial agents***
>
> *(1) A commercial agent shall not be entitled to the commission referred to in regulation 7 above if that commission is payable, by virtue of regulation 8 above, to the previous commercial agent, unless it is equitable because of the circumstances for the commission to be shared between the commercial agents.*
>
> *(2) The principal shall be liable for any sum due under paragraph (1) above to the person entitled to it in accordance with that paragraph, and any sum which the other commercial agent receives to which he is not entitled shall be refunded to the principal."*

Regulation 9 deals with the situation where a new agent is entitled to commission under Regulation 7 which the outgoing agent would be entitled to under Regulation 8. The new agent is not entitled to that commission if the old agent is entitled to it, "*unless it is equitable because of the circumstances for the commission to be shared between the commercial agents.*"

Again the Regulations leave the situation opaque; in this situation, who decides whether it is equitable to share the commission? From a commercial perspective, the principal is going to want to pay the new agent, and is unlikely to have any reason (other than to avoid a claim) to pay the old agent. Whilst this looks on the face of it to be an area ripe for dispute, in practice it has been an issue which rarely, if ever, reaches a lawyer's desk.

When is commission due to be paid?

Principals and agents often make their own agreements as to when commission is actually to be paid to the agent, and often this takes the form of a "pay when paid" clause. However, if there is no agreement on this point, Regulation 10 provides the backstop. Regulation 10 provides:

> "***10.— When commission due and date for payment***
>
> *(1) Commission shall become due as soon as, and to the extent that, one of the following circumstances occurs:*
>
> *(a) the principal has executed the transaction; or*
>
> *(b) the principal should, according to his agreement with the third party, have executed the transaction; or*
>
> *(c) the third party has executed the transaction.*
>
> *(2) Commission shall become due at the latest when the third party has executed his part of the transaction or should have done so if the principal had executed his part of the transaction, as he should have.*
>
> *(3) The commission shall be paid not later than on the last day of the month following the quarter in which it became due, and, for the purposes of these Regulations, unless otherwise agreed between the parties, the first quarter period shall run from the date the agency contract takes effect, and subsequent periods shall run from that date in the third month thereafter or the beginning of the fourth month, whichever is the sooner.*"

As noted above, commission will be due at the earliest of when the goods are delivered, on the due date for delivery, or when the customer pays. Once commission is due it must be paid in accordance with Regulation 10(3).

These issues are usually resolved commercially and it is rare that any legal dispute arises pursuant to this Regulation.

Entitlement to commission – when can it be withheld or recovered?

Regulation 11 sets out when there is an "Extinction of [the] right to commission". It states:

> "*11.— Extinction of right to commission*
>
> *(1) The right to commission can be extinguished only if and to the extent that—*
>
> *(a) it is established that the contract between the third party and the principal will not be executed; and*
>
> *(b) that fact is due to a reason for which the principal is not to blame.*
>
> *(2) Any commission which the commercial agent has already received shall be refunded if the right to it is extinguished.*
>
> *(3) Any agreement to derogate from paragraph (1) above to the detriment of the commercial agent shall be void.*"

Thus, the agent will only not be entitled to commission, or will have to repay it, if the order is cancelled and that is for "*a reason for which the principal is not to blame*". So, if the customer refuses to take delivery, or does not pay, through no fault of the principal, then no commission is payable and any commission paid can be recovered from the agent or, more likely, will be set off against future commissions or can be reclaimed.

However, if the order is cancelled because of non-delivery, late delivery or delivery of faulty goods, the agent generally remains entitled to commission.

Entitlement to commission – how can the agent check on sales?

Regulation 12 provides an agent with a right of access to information from the principal. It provides:

> "***12.— Periodic supply of information as to commission due and right of inspection of principal's books***

> *(1) The principal shall supply his commercial agent with a statement of the commission due, not later than the last day of the month following the quarter in which the commission has become due, and such statement shall set out the main components used in calculating the amount of the commission.*
>
> *(2) A commercial agent shall be entitled to demand that he be provided with all the information (and in particular an extract from the books) which is available to his principal and which he needs in order to check the amount of the commission due to him.*
>
> *(3) Any agreement to derogate from paragraphs (1) and (2) above shall be void.*
>
> *(4) Nothing in this regulation shall remove or restrict the effect of, or prevent reliance upon, any enactment or rule of law which recognises the right of an agent to inspect the books of a principal.*"

Under Regulation 12, a principal has to provide the agent with a quarterly commission statement, and, significantly, an agent can demand that the principal provides to him/her the information he needs – including extracts from the principal's books (sales ledgers, etc.) – to check the commission due. This obligation does sometimes get invoked during an agency, where the agent is sceptical it is being paid all commission due and/or the principal is not sending out regular or complete commission statements. The question however arises: how would this provision be enforced if the principal refuses to supply the requested material? A mandatory injunction may be the best route, though the cost-benefit analysis may well preclude this, and in practice this Regulation is not often invoked within the litigation context. This is largely because following termination the parties either separate amicably (or at least by consent) or enter into a dispute, during which the principal will be obliged to provide the relevant sales documentation in any event as part of the disclosure process.

CHAPTER 5A

VARYING THE AGENCY CONTRACT – PRACTICAL GUIDE TO THE OPPORTUNITIES AND RESTRICTIONS ON VARYING THE TERMS OF THE AGENCY: COMMISSION, TERRITORY, PRODUCTS, ETC.

Introduction

It will often happen that one of the parties – usually the principal – will want to vary the terms of the agency contract. Generally there will be nothing sinister afoot; simply that commercial conditions have changed, so that it makes sense to amend the product range, or the territory covered by the agent, or even the commission structure. Sometimes, the principal will feel the need to increase its profit margins by cutting the commission rates. Occasionally, a principal might even seek to goad an agent into leaving by making it more difficult to make decent money out of the agency.

There is nothing in the Regulations which attempts to deal with these situations, which means that (provided the applicable law is English law) English contract law applies, as it would to any other sort of contract. We look at this, briefly, below.

However, where the Regulations come in, is in relation to the effect of any supposed variation for the purposes of the entitlement to compensation/indemnity under Regulation 17.

Varying a contract

Parties to a contract are entitled to – and often do – decide that they would like to have different terms agreed to the ones they originally 'signed up to'. If they can agree on what the replacement terms should be, they do so and then those new terms become terms of the contract, replacing as appropriate any of the original terms. If the process is to be completed successfully, the parties are well advised to record the new terms in writing.

So far, so good.

However, things do not always happen in such an amicable and orderly way.

Oral variations

One common problem is that variations are not always written down and signed – in which case parties do not always later agree on whether a term *has* been varied, and if so how. An agent may say, for instance, that s/he only agreed to accept a reduced commission on a particular category of sale, or for a specified period; whilst the principal may claim that an agreement was reached to reduce the commission rate generally and indefinitely.

There is no easy or clever legal answer in such situations. If necessary, a court will have to decide, after hearing all the relevant evidence, who (on the balance of probabilities) has got it right.

It is worth noting in this context that if there is a written contract which says that no variations are to be made except in writing, it will be difficult to rely on any alleged oral variation.

Variations imposed unilaterally

Another even more frequent problem is that one party (nearly always the principal) will announce, rather than sit down and agree, a particular 'variation'. "From now on," for example, "we will only be paying half commission rates on items which are discounted from the standard price list"; or "From now on this particular account will be a house account". What is the situation if the agent does not agree to the change, but does not leave in protest? Has the 'variation' become agreed by default?

Again, there is often no easy answer. Much will depend on the reaction of the other party (in the above examples, the agent) at the time. At one extreme, the agent might attend a sales meeting at which the change is announced and say nothing when asked whether s/he objects. At the other extreme, the agent might instruct a solicitor to send a letter protesting the change and demanding the balance of the commission that would have been paid but for the change, and reserving the agent's right to sue for it if it remains unpaid.

The test is:

- If, by the agent's conduct (including words, oral or written), s/he demonstrates that s/he is not accepting the change, then it will not be binding on him/her – in which case a principal who unilaterally implements the change anyway will be liable for an accruing debt of unpaid commission.

- However, if the agent's conduct does not demonstrate non-acceptance, then in practice, by continuing to work under the varied terms (a newly implemented commission structure, for instance), the agent will normally have done enough to persuade the courts that, however reluctantly, s/he agreed to varying the agency contract in that way.

In short, the onus is very much on the party on whom the 'variation' was imposed to make it clear that they do not accept it.

Tip for agent: If your principal tries to impose a change to the terms of the agency which you do not want to accept, register your protest clearly in writing. Bear in mind that a principal may be willing to make a payment in return for a variation that is to its advantage but your disadvantage.

Tips for principal: There is no right unilaterally to change the terms of an agency contract. If you want to change the terms of an agency, make sure you get the agent's consent, preferably in writing. Be prepared for a commercial negotiation – the agent may well seek a quid pro quo. Be aware that if the agent protests the change, it may well not serve to vary the original terms of the agency.

Effect of variation – is it a termination?

One very important issue sometimes arises in the context of the variation of an agency contract: does it amount to a termination, or 'partial termination' of the contract?

Example 1:- The agent sells the principal's products in two territories: Western England and Wales. One or other party (perhaps both) want to remove Wales from the agency. Is that a variation of the agency contract, or the termination of that agency contract and the replacement of it with another?

Example 2:- An agent sells women's clothing for a principal. The principal also manufactures men's clothing. The principal wants the agent to take on the men's range as well. Is that a new (second) agency, or simply a variation to the original agency? And if, some years later, the principal ceases to manufacture men's clothing, does that constitute only the termination of the new men's agency, or the termination of the larger, varied agency contract for both men's and women's?

The reason the issue is so important is that a variation will not give rise to an entitlement to compensation/indemnity, whereas a termination might well do.

So, to the examples.

Example 1: The first point to make is: there is no such thing as a 'partial termination' – either a contract is terminated or it is not.

There is nothing to stop the parties agreeing to remove Wales from the scope of the agency contract, and if they do so that would constitute a variation (and not a termination). However, what if the principal removes Wales in the teeth of the agent's protests?

What the agent can<u>not</u> do is to accept that action as terminating his agency in Wales and expect to be compensated/indemnified for his 'Welsh' agency. S/he must either (a) accept the variation; (b) protest the attempt unilaterally to vary and assert her/his right to continue to be paid commission on sales made to customers in Wales (which will in practice probably force the principal into terminating the whole agency or into withdrawing the removal of Wales); (c) treat the unilateral removal of

Wales as being an (obviously) serious breach of the agency contract and thus as terminating that agency contract so as to entitle her/him to compensation/indemnity.

Tip for agent: If your principal unilaterally reduces your product range or territory, you are not entitled to compensation/indemnity unless you resign in protest.

Legal advice warning: If this issue arises, it is probably best to seek legal advice.

Example 2: There is no clear answer to this one. It will probably depend on how the matter is dealt with by the parties at the time.

- If, for instance, a fresh contract is made for both the men's and women's ranges, then it will be an agreed variation. If later the principal removes the men's range, that will be a serious breach of that contract, entitling the agent to resign in protest.

- If, however, a new contract is issued just for the men's range (perhaps with some of the terms different to the original contact – a different commission structure, for example), then there will be two agency contracts. If the principal subsequently terminates the men's range, the agency for the women's range continues as before. (The agent will in theory be entitled to compensation/indemnity for termination of the men's agency; although if the principal has ceased to manufacture that range, the level of such compensation/indemnity might be nil).

Tip for principal: If you want to add a territory or product range, you have the option of doing so as a second agency, which gives you additional flexibility later. If you want to adopt that course, make sure there are two separate written contracts (preferably not on identical terms).

CHAPTER 5B

VARYING THE AGENCY CONTRACT – LEGAL GUIDE

As noted above, the relevant law applicable to contractual variations is general contract law; it does not derive from the Regulations. Further, the issue of variation is not one that has been dealt with to any large degree in the commercial agency cases.

There are however some fundamental principles that need to be borne in mind when considering variations:

1. As with any agreement, in the case of a commercial agency arrangement, the first place to look will be the contract (if there is a written contract), which may say in what circumstances the parties can vary the contract and, importantly, how they should go about any variation. It is very important that any contractual formalities to vary a contract are followed. For example, if the contract says the parties can only effect a variation in writing signed by the parties, any informal variation is likely to be ineffective.[68] That said, if the parties act on a variation that has not been made in accordance with the contract's variation formalities, an estoppel might arise preventing a party from denying the variation by relying on those formalities.

2. Some contracts will contain a unilateral right of variation in favour of the principal. However, if there is a unilateral right to vary in favour of the principal then it is appears likely, based on the non-agency case of *Nash and others v Paragon Finance Plc,*[69] and the underlying purpose of the Regulations, that the court will

68 *Rock Advertising Ltd v MWB Business Exchange Centres Ltd* [2018] UKSC 24. Parties should also ensure that, unless the variation is by deed, consideration is given for the variation.

69 [2001] EWCA Civ 1466

imply a term that such a right must not be exercised capriciously, arbitrarily or for an improper purpose.

3. In the absence of an express contractual right, unilateral variation is not permitted; neither party can force on the other a change to their contract without agreement and to seek to do so would be a breach of contract. Any significant variation imposed unilaterally would be likely to give grounds for the other party to terminate the contract – and, if the innocent party is the agent, to claim compensation/indemnity.

4. If the contract is silent about variations or there is no written contract, any variation must be agreed and must be supported by consideration (as is also the case for varying a written contract, though consideration is not required for variations effected by deed). Agreement to the variation could be evidenced by conduct.

CHAPTER 6A

TERMINATION OF THE AGENCY – PRACTICAL GUIDE

Practical guide to how an agency can be terminated and what the effects are of different ways of terminating and of the different reasons for terminating.

Introduction

All things come to an end, and agency contracts are no exception.

Sometimes the end will be planned and amicable (agreed date for retirement; the parties wanting to go their different ways, etc.). At others it will be sudden and acrimonious (the principal being dissatisfied with its agent's lack of results, or wanting to cut out the agent's increasing commission earnings once the market has been established; the agent frustrated by his/her principal's failure to pay commissions as it ought, or to provide the necessary tools for the job). Not unusually, a termination will begin fairly amicably, but will quickly descend into acrimony when the agent presses for compensation or an indemnity to which the principal does not feel the agent ought to be entitled.

At the end of the day, one question usually comes to dominate: Was the termination such that the agent is entitled to claim compensation/indemnity, or not? It is that question that this chapter will address. (The next chapter focusses on the related question: how much?)

Overview of when compensation/indemnity is payable

The basic position is that compensation/indemnity is payable unless the agent has freely chosen to leave the agency, or has behaved so badly that the principal was entitled to require him/her to leave.

Thus compensation/indemnity is payable when:

- The principal terminates the agency contract, other than because of the agent's serious breach of it.

- A fixed-term agency contract expires.
- The agent becomes too ill to continue.
- The agent retires at a suitable age for retirement.
- The agent terminates the agency contract because of the principal's serious breach of it.

Compensation/indemnity is not payable when:

- The agent chooses to leave the agency, other than because of the principal's serious breach of it.
- The agent has been in serious breach of the agency contract and the principal has terminated it for that reason.
- The agent has chosen, with the principal's consent, to assign the agency contract to another agent (presumably for a sum of money, but conceivably to a friend/relative without payment).

Termination for fault

The rules (law) applying to situations where one party to an agency contract terminates it on the supposed basis that the other party has been in serious breach – or at least seeks to defend a more neutral termination on that basis subsequently – are no different to the rules (law) applying to any other sort of commercial contract under English law.

Those rules are:-

- *The breach must be of sufficient seriousness*, or there must be a series of breaches amounting in combination to a serious failure to comply with the terms of the contract (see Chapter 3 on Rights and Duties for examples of what sort of breach(es) might fall into this category).
- *The party who terminates must do so fairly promptly*; they must not continue to perform the agency contract after knowing of the breach. If a party waits too long before terminating, they will lose the right in law to terminate because of that breach.

- *The party who terminates must do so because of the breach* and not for another unrelated reason.

As one might imagine, arguments often arise on one, two or all three of these points. Each situation must be judged on its own facts, but here are a couple of case studies modified from real life situations, which illustrate some of the relevant issues.

Case study 1

There is a written agency contract which sets out in an appendix an annual target volume of sales. In the contract there is a term that says that failure to meet the target amounts to a serious breach entitling the principal to terminate. The agent does not quite meet the target in the first year, but the principal does nothing and the agency continues. The principal sets a higher target for the second year. Half way through the second year, sales are 25% behind target. Can the principal terminate?

If the principal terminates at this point, there are several potential problems for the principal. First, the target is an annual one and the year is only half over; strictly, there has not yet been any breach of the requirement to reach the target in that year. Secondly, the principal cannot now rely on the failure to meet the target in the first year; if it wanted to do so, it would have had to terminate at the end of the first year – it is too late now. Thirdly, it is not clear whether the target for the second year was set in such a way as to create an obligation on the agent to meet it. Unless the contract provides for a way of adjusting targets (up to 75% of the previous year's actual sales, for instance), it should be assumed that the target must either remain unchanged or must be agreed as reasonable by both parties if adjusted. In this case the agent would probably not have agreed that it was reasonable to raise the target significantly when the previous year's target was not met.

Better for the principal to write to the agent along the lines: 'You are on course to miss this year's target by a significant margin. We did not enforce the obligation last year because the target was almost reached; but we shall have to enforce it this year. It was set as a reasonable target given that ... You made no objection to it as a reasonable target. If you do not meet it, we intend to terminate the contract at the end of the year'. If the agent responds saying that the target was always unreasonable and he/she did object or at least did not agree, then at least the principal knows where it stands and can take a view on whether it can demonstrate that the target was reasonable and/or agreed. If the agent does not respond in those terms, then summary termination and avoiding paying compensation or an indemnity may be possible at the end of the year, though as each case turns on its facts, caution should be exercised.

Case study 2

There is short written agency contract which appoints an agent to sell the principal's products in the UK. After some years, the principal decides that it can better sell a particular part of its product range directly rather than through the agent. It raises this with the agent in December and says it will continue to pay commissions on those sales for three months after it takes over responsibility for them in the new year. The agent argues that the proposed change should not happen. From January the principal does take over responsibility for sales of that part of the range and does pay the agent commission on those sales for January – March, but then stops. Can the agent terminate once the principal ceases to pay commission?

The potential problems for the agent if they terminate at this point are these. First, did the agent's conduct taken as a whole amount to an acceptance of a variation to the agency contract? Although the agent objected to the proposal, he/she did not say that they would treat the agency contract as terminated if it was implemented; moreover, he/she accepted the commission for three months on sales made by the principal directly. Secondly, if (as is not unlikely, depending on the evidence of the agent's objections in December) there was *no* variation, is it too late for the agent to terminate the agency because of a breach that took effect three months ago? On the one hand, it is true that the principal implemented the proposal it had made from the start of January; on the other, it could well be argued that there was no actual breach of the agency contract for so long as the principal continued to pay commission on the relevant sales.

If the agent does wish to terminate, they should write to the principal in these terms: 'As you know, I was opposed to the change in product range and never agreed to it. I was prepared to continue the agency so long as I wasn't going to lose commission, but unless you pay me April's commission within 14 days, I will be forced to conclude that you do not intend to abide by the terms of our contract and will have to terminate the agency.' If the principal responds claiming the agent did agree to the change, then the agent will be able to assess that claim on its merits; if the principal does not respond in that way (and it may well not – instead simply seeking to justify the change), then the agent will probably be able to terminate and still claim compensation/indemnity.

Tip for agents and principals concerning termination for fault:-

As should be clear, every situation will turn on its own facts, but here are some generic, practical suggestions to assist in steering a successful course:

1) If you are getting to the point where you are considering terminating, set out in writing to the other party what the problem is and why it is serious. If there is a written contract, you might be able to point to a specific provision which you say the other party has breached. Also, or alternatively, you might be able to point to an obligation under Regulation 3 or Regulation 4 which you say has been breached.

2) If it is a continuing problem (failing to turn up for meetings, failing to pay commission on time, etc.), you may be able/want to warn the other party that unless it addresses the problem, you will be forced to consider terminating – you may even give a deadline for addressing the problem.

3) If it is a one-off breach (a principal hiding a large sale to a particular customer to avoid paying commission, an agent behaving very inappropriately to a customer, etc.) you must either decide to terminate pretty much as soon as you find out about it, or at least make it clear that you may well do so pending a meeting, response to a letter, etc., to give the other party an opportunity to give their side of the story.

4) When you terminate, say clearly that you are doing so because of the action(s) you believe amounted to a serious breach of the agency contract.

Legal advice warning: If this issue arises, it is best to seek legal advice if you have the opportunity/means.

Expiry of a fixed term agency contract

If the fixed term is permitted to expire, it is treated as if the principal had given notice of termination. Compensation/indemnity is payable.

Age, ill-health and death

The first point to make is: *a company cannot become old or ill.* That is one of the potential disadvantages of incorporation by a sole trader. If an agent, having incorporated a company and contracted with principals as the company, becomes too ill to continue the agency, or reaches a suitable age and wants to retire, there will no entitlement to compensation/indemnity. That said, even where an agency contract is between a principal and a corporate agent, the individual(s) running the agency are often the asset the principal wished at the outset to appoint. If such individuals did wish to retire, they could approach the principal and explain that they were planning to hand the company over to a new person to run the agency company. In such circumstances there is a strong possibility that a principal would refuse, on the basis that the contract was, effectively, a personal contract. In that event, the agent could, in effect, compel the principal to terminate the agency; or obtain a written confirmation from the principal that it considers the individual running the agent is in reality 'the agent'. In the latter case the agent may then have an argument that if that individual retires, compensation or an indemnity should be paid. This approach has not been tested in the courts and it is uncertain how the courts would deal with such a case, but there are clearly arguments on both sides.

Tip for agent: don't incorporate if you want to protect yourself against ill-health/retirement.

Retirement

When is an agent old enough to retire? Surprisingly perhaps, there is no clear answer. The legal test is: when the agent *"cannot reasonably be required to continue"*. Certainly state retirement age at the relevant time would be old enough. We would have thought that 65 or over would be old enough. Under 60 and healthy? Probably not old enough. Between 60 and 65? Unclear; it might depend on what sort of agency and what level of health the agent has.

Another potentially relevant factor (as would be the case if ill-health is the reason for leaving) is whether the agent wishes to retain other agencies. If so, the case for being sufficiently old becomes potentially harder to establish.

Tip for agent: if you wish to terminate an agency in order to retire, it's best to discuss that with your principal well in advance and secure its consent to your retirement if possible.

Tip for principal: if an agent wants to retire but you don't believe the agent's age justifies that, say so – and why – in writing before the termination occurs.

Ill health

This is more straightforward. If an agent's state of health presents a genuine impediment to being able to carry out the agency duties, the agent may terminate the agency contract and remain entitled to compensation/indemnity.

Note, it may be that a particular health issue prevents an agent continuing to act for one principal, but not for others (e.g. if the problematic agency requires heavy lifting, or much longer driving distances).

Tip for agent: if you wish to terminate an agency on grounds of health, try to get some medical evidence – a GP's letter should suffice – before you do so. Set out in writing to your principal what the issue is and provide a copy of any medical evidence.

Death

If an agent dies whilst still engaged as an agent, their estate becomes entitled to compensation or an indemnity. It is prudent for agents to make relevant family member(s) aware of that fact.

'Termination' by assignment

If an agent is entitled to assign the agency (transfer the rights and obligations to another person or company) – either because it is provided for in the agency contract, or because the principal agrees to it – then the agency continues as before, on the same terms. There is, in law, no 'termination' at all; simply the continuation of it with a new agent.

Time limit

Finally, but very importantly, the entitlement to compensation/indemnity is lost if the principal is not notified within **one year or termination** that the agent (or his/her estate) intends pursuing that entitlement. A letter or email would suffice – even a phone call in theory (although proving the latter makes it a risky means of communication).

The agent does not actually have to sue the principal within one year, simply notify it that he/she is entitled to be paid compensation/indemnity.

CHAPTER 6B

TERMINATION OF THE AGENCY – LEGAL GUIDE

Regulations 15, 16 and 18

Notice periods

Most contracts provide for notice periods. However, the Regulations provide default, mandatory minimum notice periods which apply:

1. In the event that the contract between agent and principal does not contain a term relating to notice periods; or
2. If the agency contract provides for a notice period shorter than those provided for in the Regulations.

These notice periods are set out in Regulation 15, which provides:

> "*(1) Where an agency contract is concluded for an indefinite period either party may terminate it by notice.*
>
> *(2) The period of notice shall be—*
>
> *(a) 1 month for the first year of the contract;*
>
> *(b) 2 months for the second year commenced;*
>
> *(c) 3 months for the third year commenced and for the subsequent years;*
>
> *and the parties may not agree on any shorter periods of notice.*
>
> *(3) If the parties agree on longer periods than those laid down in paragraph (2) above, the period of notice to be observed by the principal must not be shorter than that to be observed by the commercial agent.*
>
> *(4) Unless otherwise agreed by the parties, the end of the period of notice must coincide with the end of a calendar month.*

> *(5) The provisions of this regulation shall also apply to an agency contract for a fixed period where it is converted under regulation 14 above into an agency contract for an indefinite period subject to the proviso that the earlier fixed period must be taken into account in the calculation of the period of notice."*

In line with the Directive's objective to protect commercial agents, this Regulation expressly provides that the parties may not agree shorter periods of notice. However, Regulation 15(3) makes it clear that the parties can agree a longer notice period and if they do, the period of notice that the principal is entitled to cannot be longer than that to which the agent is entitled.

Accordingly, Regulation 15 operates to provide a minimum level of protection to an agent that cannot be excluded by the parties.

It is also noteworthy that Regulation 15 provides that (unless otherwise agreed by the parties) the end of the period of notice must coincide with the end of the calendar month. This means that if the contract is terminated in the middle of one month, the notice period will in effect be lengthened by two weeks. So if the notice is given on 15 March, and the agent is entitled to 3 months' notice pursuant to Regulation 15, the notice period will end on 30 June (i.e. 3.5 months after termination).

It is very often the case that Regulation 15 is not properly observed by principals, who do not give sufficient notice. In such circumstances the agent will have a claim against the principal for breach of Regulation 15.

But what is that claim for? The amount due to the agent is damages for the relevant period; i.e. the net commission it would have made during the period of notice after the agent's costs have been subtracted. Normally, it is inappropriate for the agent to receive of gross commissions in circumstances where the agent is no longer incurring expenses in generating that commission. However, if the contract is terminated with immediate effect, the agent may still have overheads to service in circumstances where a source of income has been cut off with insufficient notice, and therefore, the payment should take this into account. That said, in many cases, principals and agents come to an agreement as to payments in lieu of notice (though the Regulations make no provision for such payments).

Termination by the agent

Clearly it is open to an agent to bring the agency contract to an end. However, under Regulation 18(b) the agent will lose the right to an indemnity or compensation if it does so unless the agency is brought to an end because of the agent's age or ill health, or because the principal has committed a repudiatory breach of the agency contract.

This is set out in Regulation 18, which provides:

> "*The indemnity or compensation referred to in regulation 17 above shall not be payable to the commercial agent where—*
>
> *(a) the principal has terminated the agency contract because of default attributable to the commercial agent which would justify immediate termination of the agency contract pursuant to regulation 16 above; or*
>
> *(b) the commercial agent has himself terminated the agency contract, unless such termination is justified—*
>
> *(i) by circumstances attributable to the principal, or*
>
> *(ii) on grounds of the age, infirmity or illness of the commercial agent in consequence of which he cannot reasonably be required to continue his activities; or*
>
> *(c) the commercial agent, with the agreement of his principal, assigns his rights and duties under the agency contract to another person.*"

Termination by agent justified by circumstances attributable to the principal

Regulation 18(b)(i) enables the agent to terminate the agency contract and remain entitled to a Regulation 17 payment if the agent's termination is justified by "*circumstances attributable to the principal*".

Whilst the formulation "*circumstances attributable to the principal*" is slightly odd, in effect it mirrors the employment law concept of constructive dismissal or the common law position where a party is able to accept the other party's repudiatory breach of contract, thereby bringing the contract to an end, and sue for damages. Thus, if the principal commits a fundamental breach of contract, the agent will be entitled to bring the contract to an end and claim a Regulation 17 payment.

What amounts to a repudiatory breach of contract will depend on the facts of each case, and it can be a difficult call. For a breach to be repudiatory, it has to be such that a reasonable person in the position of the innocent party would conclude that the contract-breaker had clearly shown an intention to abandon and altogether refuse to perform the contract.

A further issue to consider for agents considering terminating their agreements in reliance on Regulation 18(b)(i): the decision to terminate following the principal's breach(es) needs to be made relatively promptly following discovery of the principal's breach(es). This is because the doctrines of waiver and affirmation will apply. Whilst those principles will not be analysed in detail here, in summary, when a repudiatory breach has taken place, the wronged party has a choice between continuing with the contract or bringing it to an end. In both cases the wronged party can sue for damages, but clearly, in a commercial agency situation, if the contract is ongoing, Regulation 18(b)(i) cannot bite and the agent cannot claim a Regulation 17 payment.

Whilst the wronged party has some time to consider its position, it will need to move promptly (and protect its position in the meantime by reserving its rights in respect of the breach with the party in breach). Alacrity is required as a wronged party can be taken to have waived the breach and affirmed the contract by continuing to act as if bound by the contract (i.e. by continuing to perform its obligations and to call for performance by the party in breach). Accepting the status quo for too long could be fatal for an agent's claim. Furthermore, waiting too long and then purporting to terminate when the entitlement has evaporated will leave the agent in repudiatory breach of contract and the principal may, as a result, bring the contract to an end and avoid liability under Regulation 17.

This issue arose in *Bell Electric v Aweco Appliance Systems GmBH & Co KG.*[70] In that case, the principal stopped paying commissions, without

70 [2002] EWHC 872

explanation to the agent, and then unilaterally sought to impose different contractual terms upon the agent.

The court held that the continued failure to pay commissions was a repudiatory breach (but noted that a single failure to pay would not have been). The court also held that the unilateral attempt to impose new terms (and the concordant refusal by the principal to abide by the existing contract) was also repudiatory conduct.

After the breaches had taken place, and after issuing (but not serving) court proceedings against the principal, the agent continued to act as the principal's agent, as during that period he and the principal were in discussions about a way forward. However, the agent eventually served the proceedings and informed the principal that he was bringing the contract to an end.

One of the issues in the case was whether the agent had waived the breaches and affirmed the contract. If he had, he would have no entitlement to damages at common law or a Regulation 17 payment. The agent sought to rely on a breach which took place on 31 October 2000. On 7 and 14 November 2000, the agent went to meetings and he wrote reports relating to those meetings on 15 and 16 November 2000, (which conduct the court held to evidence performance of the contract). The agent then sought to accept the principal's breach on 17 November 2000. The court found that the agent had not in fact affirmed the contract, on the basis that before the agent attended the meetings, he had made it clear to the principal that he was considering his position as to a possible change to his relationship with his principal. In effect, the court held that he had reserved his position and his conduct in accordance with the contract following the 31 October breach was "*consistent with an intention to perform the contract only pending a decision whether to accept the compromise or not.*" The court held that during this period, "*no action on his part could be seen as constituting an intention to affirm the contract and to give up his right to discharge the contract by relying upon the earlier repudiatory breaches*".

The agent was therefore entitled to damages for breach of contract and was, alternatively, entitled to compensation under Regulation 17. It is of note that the Court concluded that Regulation 18(b)(i) (and 18(a), discussed below):

> "*...ought to be seen as the reverse sides of the same coin. In other words, the compensation is not payable if the principal terminates in circumstances which would be justifiable at common law because of the agent's conduct; but on the other hand it is payable if the commercial agent terminates in circumstances which are justifiable at common law because of the conduct of the principal. In either case, if the innocent party affirms the contract and precludes the right to rely on the repudiatory breach, the attempt thereafter to terminate the contract, absent some fresh repudiatory breach, will not be justifiable within the meaning of the regulations.*"

On grounds of age or ill health

Under Regulation 18(b)(ii), an agent remains entitled to compensation or an indemnity if they bring the contract to an end "*on grounds of the age, infirmity or illness of the commercial agent in consequence of which he cannot reasonably be required to continue his activities*".

As has been seen in Chapter 6A when considering the practical impact of the Regulations, whilst only an individual agent, rather than a company, can get ill or old and thus these provisions, on their face, do not apply to agents that are corporate entities, resourceful agents may be able to find a way around this difficulty.

As has also been seen in Chapter 6A, an area of uncertainty that arises under Regulation 18(b)(ii) is that the Regulations do not set out when an agent will reach an age where he "*cannot reasonably be required to continue his activities*". This uncertainty is reinforced as, in the UK, there is no default retirement age. This uncertainty has been the subject of commentary and analysis in the courts.

One textbook suggests that the wording of Regulation 18(b)(ii) is such that the agent can only benefit from compensation or an indemnity if he can no longer work "*on grounds of… age, infirmity or illness*" due to incapacity; that is, there is no retirement age and the agent must continue for as long as he/she is physically able.[71] This effectively rewrites the provision with "and" instead of "or" and seems wrong. Also, given that one of the main purposes of the Regulations is to protect agents, this interpretation seems unlikely, as it would put an agent in a worse position than most of the population.

In *Abbot v Condici*,[72] the court interpreted the provision differently and held that although there might be exceptional cases, in general an agent could not reasonably be required to continue his/her activities beyond what was recognised as his appropriate retirement age. The court found that the age of 65 was a reasonable age for an agent to retire and remain entitled to a post-termination payment under the Regulations, as the age of 65 was "*embedded as a retirement milestone*".

That case was decided before the default retirement age of 65 was abolished in April 2011 and it is questionable whether the age of 65 would be considered an appropriate age for the retirement of an agent who wishes to obtain the benefit of Regulation 18(b)(ii). Further, as the retirement age for the age of the state pension creeps up, it is suspected that so would the age of retirement deemed such that the agent "*cannot reasonably be required to continue his activities*" under Regulation 18(b)(ii).

That said, the abolition of the retirement age was intended to prevent discrimination by an employer based on a person's age by preventing the employer from dismissing them solely because of their age. Clearly, that is not directly analogous to a situation where an agent wants to retire because of her/his age.

Drawing these threads together, it would seem likely that if an agent wishes to retire at an age at least equal to the age at which s/he is entitled to a state pension, then an entitlement to compensation/indemnity will apply.

Clearly from an agent's perspective, they will wish to retain their right to indemnity or compensation and retire at a reasonable age to enjoy the benefit of their work. From the principal's perspective, they may baulk

71 Saintier and Scholes, LLP 2005.

72 [2005] 2 Lloyd's Rep 450

at giving an ageing agent an expensive golden goodbye. Managing the legal issues, as well as the relationship issues that go hand-in-hand with an agent's retirement, can be tricky, and principals and agents are well advised to think carefully before taking any steps, lest they compromise their position or surrender any rights.

The issue of whether an agent can reasonably be required to continue her/his activities on grounds of infirmity or illness have not been before the courts and the Regulations provide no insight into what these provisions mean in practice. As such, principals and agents should consider the practical matters discussed in this respect in in Chapter 6A.

Termination by principal

Clearly it is open to a principal to terminate an agency agreement at any time. However, in doing so without careful consideration, they will risk claims by the agent for breach of contract and under the Regulations.

Termination by principal because the agent has breached the terms of the agency

Regulation 18(a) provides that:

> "*The indemnity or compensation referred to in regulation 17 above shall not be payable to the commercial agent where—*
>
> *(a) the principal has terminated the agency contract because of default attributable to the commercial agent which would justify immediate termination of the agency contract pursuant to regulation 16 above*"

The relevant part of Regulation 16 for these purposes provides:

> "*These Regulations shall not affect the application of any enactment or rule of law which provides for the immediate termination of the agency contract—*
>
> *(a) because of the failure of one party to carry out all or part of his obligations under that contract*".

In *Bell v Aweco*,[73] the court held that the effect of Regulation 16(a) and 18(a) was that compensation or indemnity payments will not be payable to an agent if the principal terminates the agreement "*in circumstances which would be justifiable at common law because of the agent's conduct*".

This means that if an agent is in repudiatory breach of contract, the principal may accept that breach, bring the contract to an end and avoid making a Regulation 17 payment. However, as ever, parties must be alive to the issues of waiver and affirmation; a repudiation which is not accepted is famously a 'thing writ in water'.

What constitutes a repudiatory breach can, however, be difficult to assess, as is illustrated by the cases considered below.

In *Crocs Europe BV v Craig Lee & Anor trading as Spectrum Agencies (a partnership)*,[74] (which is considered in Chapter 4B in the context of the legal status of Regulation 3) one of the agent's employees posted spoof derogatory comments about its principal, Crocs, on a web-page to which they sent a link to certain of their own staff and other friends in the business, which was headed "That's a Croc!! Of Sh**e!!".

Crocs terminated the agency on the basis that the comments amounted to a breach of contract, and argued that it was entitled to terminate the agency without paying compensation as a result of the agent's breach under Regulation 18(a).

Whilst the court held that the agent's conduct did constitute a breach of its obligations to look after the interests of the principal and to act dutifully and in good faith, it concluded that the agent had not lost its entitlement to post-termination compensation because the breach was not sufficiently serious to justify termination.

The court emphasised that there was no evidence of harm suffered by Crocs as a result of the comments, but it was noted by one judge that the breach was "*quite close to the borderline*".

---

73 [2002] EWHC 872

74 [2012] EWCA Civ 1400

In *Cooper and others v Pure Fishing (UK) Limited,*[75] (which is considered in Chapter 4B in respect of Regulation 4 and the principal's duty of good faith to its agent) the agent refused to market a new range of products introduced by the principal, Pure Fishing. The agent believed that the new products competed with the products sold by another of its principals.

Subsequently, Pure Fishing informed the agent that it would not be renewing the agency agreement when it expired as a result of the agent's refusal to market the new products, which it asserted amounted to a breach of contract. Pure Fishing also argued that, as a result of the breach, the agent would not be entitled to compensation at the expiry of the fixed term, which is contrary to established law which provides that compensation is payable at the expiry of a fixed term.

The High Court found that the agent was entitled to compensation because the principal had not terminated the agreement because of the alleged breaches (rather, it had simply let the agency expire), and also, that the alleged breaches did not justify termination, on the basis that the principal had in effect engineered the situation with an ulterior motive, to replace its agents with employed staff. (On appeal, the Court of Appeal upheld that decision on the first ground and did not consider the seriousness of the breach.)

In *Nigel Fryer Joinery Services Limited v Ian Firth Hardware Limited,*[76] the agent was required, under the agency agreement, to work exclusively for the principal and to notify its principal if it took on work for third parties; and to submit regular reports detailing its activities. The agent took on work for another company without telling the principal, which equated to 30% of his working time; he also repeatedly failed to submit reports, despite receiving written warnings from the principal. As a consequence, the principal terminated the agreement for cause.

---

75 [2004] EWCA Civ 375

76 [2008] EWHC 767 Ch

When the agent claimed compensation, the principal fought the claim on the basis that no compensation was payable as a result of the agent's breaches of contract.

The court agreed with the principal. It found that termination would not have been justified if the agent's failure to submit reports had not been preceded by earlier breaches; an individual instance of failing to provide reports would not have been sufficient, but repeated breaches were. In the circumstances of that particular agency, where the agent agreed to work exclusively for the principal, the court held that accepting another role occupying the agent for 30% of his working time was also a repudiatory breach.

The court noted that if there has been a breach which justifies termination, this will only exclude the agent's entitlement to compensation if this breach is the ground relied upon for termination, as it was in this case.

This last point is important. Principals often terminate agency agreements for business reasons (i.e. they have cemented relationships with customers brought to them by the agent and wish to avoid the ongoing obligation to pay commissions), oblivious to the consequences that may flow from the termination. When they realise the consequences, they may seek to retrospectively justify termination on the basis of alleged breaches of contract. However, the courts have held that the termination must be "*because of*"[77] the breaches, and so the principal will need to show that at the time of the termination, the breaches were the reason for termination. In *Volvo Car Germany GmbH v Autohof Weidensdorf GmbH*,[78] the European Court of Justice, as it then was, referring to Article 18(a) of the Directive (which is mirrored in the Regulations) said:

> "*The use, by the European Union legislature, of the wording 'because of' tends to support the proposition, put forward inter alia by the Commission, that the legislature intended to require that there be a direct causal link between the default attributable to the commercial*

77 As noted above, Regulation 18(a) relieves the principal of the obligation to pay compensation or an indemnity where "*...the principal has terminated the agency contract because of default attributable to the commercial agent which would justify immediate termination of the agency...*"

78 Case C-203/09

> *agent and the principal's decision to terminate the contract in order to deprive the commercial agent of the indemnity provided for in Article 17 of the Directive.*
>
> *... "Moreover, as an exception to the agent's entitlement to an indemnity, Article 18(a) of the Directive must be interpreted restrictively. That provision cannot, therefore, be interpreted in a way which amounts to adding a ground for exclusion of the indemnity where no express provision is made to that effect."*

What this means in practice is that it is not good enough for a principal to show that before the contract was terminated the agent had been in breach of contract; the principal must show that the reason for the termination was the breach. If the principal has limited evidence that it was concerned about the alleged breaches, it will face an uphill struggle in convincing the court that he terminated because of the breaches. Significantly, in the Nigel Fryer case referred to above, the court said "*the existence of repudiatory conduct on the part of Mr Fryer* [the agent] *does not disentitle him to seek compensation under reg.18 unless it was the ground relied upon for terminating the contract.*" In that case, the court found that the breaches were the reason for the termination, and based this decision on an analysis of the letter of termination.

In *John Harold Crane v Sky In-Home Service Limited, The Secretary of State for Trade and Industry*[79] the court accepted the principal's case that it had terminated because of the agent's breach and therefore could rely on Regulation 18(a), but again emphasised "*the need to show, under reg 18(a) that the contract was terminated "because of" the qualifying breach*".

However, in the *Crocs* case referred to above, although the agent won, the court held that a principal is entitled to terminate an agency "*because of*" a particular breach, even if its motive in doing so was unconnected with that breach. A principal is permitted to act opportunistically in such circumstances (as, of course, is an agent if the positions are reversed).

79 [2007] EWHC 66 (Ch)

What happens if a principal terminates the agency agreement for business reasons, but after it has done so, finds out that an agent was in repudiatory breach before termination? Can it rely on that breach to avoid paying compensation?

This question came before the ECJ in the *Volvo*[80] case referred to above, and the court's answer was no:

> "*...when the Principal becomes aware of the commercial agents default only after the end of the contract it is no longer possible to apply the mechanism provided for in article 18(a)... the commercial agent cannot be deprived of his entitlement to an indemnity under that provision when the principal establishes after notifying him of the termination of the contract... a default on the part of the agent which was such to justify immediate termination of that contract.*"

This decision contradicts the English common law position, to the extent that a party may justify his refusal to perform a contract if there were at the time facts in existence which would have provided a good reason, provided he did not know that at the time of his refusal.[81]

This could have harsh consequences for a principal. For example, it is clearly possible that a principal terminates without giving a reason and subsequently finds that the agent had, during the term of the agency contract, been committing fraud. In such circumstances, how can it be right that the agent would still have a good claim for compensation or indemnity (even if the principal may have its own counterclaim for damages as a result of the fraud)?

This situation has been considered by the courts, though not answered definitively; whilst the agent's entitlement to compensation or an indemnity would remain in principle, such a scenario could be reflected in the amount of the payment the agent is awarded by the court, as discussed in the chapter on post-termination payments that follows.

---

80 Case C-203/09

81 See, for example, *Boston Deep Sea Fishing and Ice Co v Ansell* (1888) 39 ChD 339

Termination by assignment

An agent will be entitled to assign the agency contract to another agent if the principal consents and/or if the agency contract provides that this is possible.

However, if an agent assigns their agency contract, they will not be entitled to compensation or an indemnity, because of Regulation 18(c), which provides:

> "*The indemnity or compensation referred to in regulation 17 above shall not be payable to the commercial agent where*
>
> *(c) the commercial agent, with the agreement of his principal, assigns his rights and duties under the agency contract to another person.*"

In *Rossetti Marketing Limited, Solutions Marketing Limited v Diamond Sofa Company Limited,*[82] (which is considered in Chapter 4B in the context of an agent's duties and the issue of acting for competing principals) the Court of Appeal briefly considered the legal effect of one agent replacing another, with the principal's consent. The court concluded:[83]

> "*...reg. 18(c) clearly envisages that, where a principal agrees to instruct a new agent in place of an existing agent, in circumstances where the existing agent has transferred the agency business to the new agent, the new agent is to be treated as having taken an assignment of the existing agent's rights and duties. The fact that the common law might treat the new agency as a new contract is neither here nor there. This conclusion appears to me to comply with the commercial purpose of the Regulations.*"

Whilst not dealt with by the Regulations, it should be noted that if an agent purports to assign its rights to another agent without the principal's consent, the agent is likely to be in breach of its obligations to the principal (it is unlikely to be acting in good faith by foisting a new agent upon the principal). In addition, the new agent's claim for compensation or an

---

82 [2012] EWCA Civ 1021

83 At paragraph 55.

indemnity upon termination is likely to fail, as was the case in *Barnett Fashion Agency Ltd v Nigel Hall Menswear Ltd.*[84]

In that case, the claimant, a fashion agency (Barnett Fashion Agency Ltd) claimed compensation from Nigel Hall Menswear, the principal, following termination of a commercial agency agreement. However, Barnett Fashion Agency Limited, the company, was not the original agent and had not entered into any agency contract with Nigel Hall Menswear. Instead, a husband and wife team, working in partnership, entered into the agency contract with Nigel Hall Menswear, and sent invoices to Nigel Hall Menswear in the name of that partnership for a number of years. The agent later started sending invoices in the name of Barnett Fashion Agency Limited, the company. After the principal, Nigel Hall Menswear, terminated the agency agreement, Barnett Fashion Agency Limited brought a claim for compensation under Regulation 17 and argued that the partnership had assigned the agency contract to the limited company.

The Judge dismissed the claim on the basis that Nigel Hall Menswear had not entered into a contract with Barnett Fashion Agency Limited. The court held that in order to achieve a situation where Nigel Hall assumed a liability to the limited company, Nigel Hall would have to be a party to a novation agreement between the partnership and the limited company. Without that agreement, Barnett Fashion Agency Limited had no contract with Nigel Hall and therefore could not have any claims arising from the termination of Nigel Hall's contract with the partnership.

That is, on the face of it, a harsh result, as the individuals operating the agency did not change; only the medium through which they operated changed. Arguably the principal became aware of this as it started receiving invoices from that different legal entity, and apparently only raised the issue in defence to a claim under the Regulations.

However, the principle upon which the decision was made appears to be sound. Otherwise, an agent could assign its agency to a third party of whom the principal has no knowledge, without the principal's consent, and that third party could, in theory, claim compensation on termination of the agency. Clearly it would be wrong for the law to enable a situation

84 [2011] EWHC 978 (QB)

in which principal is forced into contractual relations with a third party it has not freely contracted with.

CHAPTER 7A

PAYMENTS FOLLOWING TERMINATION OF THE AGENCY – PRACTICAL GUIDE

Practical guide to what an agent is entitled to on termination: notice; pipeline commissions; compensation/indemnity.

Introduction

The majority of disputes concern, or at least include, the issue of how much money should the principal pay to the agent once the agency has come to an end. That was, after all, the main political driver for the European Directive that gave us the Regulations: to ensure that agents throughout the EU had similar monetary entitlements on termination.

Some of those entitlements depend on how and why the agency contract was terminated; others do not.

The most valuable right (if it exists) is generally to compensation or indemnity. The method of calculating that right remains often controversial.

Notice

As explained above, the Regulations provide for minimum periods of notice (1 month to start with; 2 months after a year; 3 months after 2 or more years – in each case ending at the end of a calendar month if the agency contract does not say differently). Of course, the agency contract might provide for a longer period of notice, in which case that longer period applies.

The right to be given notice – and both parties to the agency have the same rights under the Regulations – does not always apply. Leaving aside the relatively rare circumstances where a party (usually the agent) simply cannot provide notice – because, for example, the agent has died or suddenly become too ill to continue the agency – the main situation where a party does not have to provide notice is when summary termination is justified because of the serious breach of the other party (see chapter 6A and 6B for when that arises).

So if, for example, the principal discovers that the agent is selling competing products, or the agent's demands for payment of commission owing are rebuffed, then the wronged party can simply terminate the agency without any notice (in practice by letter or email, explaining why that action is being taken).

If the right to notice does apply and the party terminating does not provide notice, or does not provide the amount of notice it should, then the other party (in practice, almost always the agent) can claim for any loss caused by the failure to give full notice.

An example: *The agency began just over 2 years ago. There is no agency contract. The principal terminates on January 3rd giving notice to the end of the month.* The proper period of notice would end at the end of the calendar month 3 months later: i.e. **30 April.** If there had been an agency contract providing for 3 months' notice (with no mention of it having to end at the end of a calendar month), the proper period of notice would have ended 3 April.

Measure of loss

If a party is not given the full lawful period of notice, it is only any consequent actual loss for which it can claim. So in the example given just above, for example, it is the net loss of earnings that the agent would have accrued between 1 February and 30 April that is the measure of his/her loss.

In calculating the net loss, the following needs to be considered:-

1) It is the actual loss of commission during that period that provides the starting point. In other words, if it is possible to show that during the period in question the agent's commission earnings would have been lower or higher than average (as might well be the case if the agency concerned the selling of a product range which changed at least once a year), then it is the actual anticipated lost commission during the particular

period in question, and not the average monthly commission, which matters.

2) The lost commission must be calculated net of expenses. Thus if the agent has lost £1,000 anticipated commission earnings, but saved £300 in expenses, then the agent's lost commission is £700 (not £1,000).

3) The party who is complaining of a loss must give credit for any money received during the relevant period, which would not have been received had proper notice been given. So in the example above, if the agent secures a replacement agency on 1 April and earns at least as much commission in April as s/he would have earned in the original agency, then loss can only be claimed until 31 March.

Pipeline commission

The Regulations provide that an agent is entitled to be paid commissions on transactions which conclude (sales of products delivered and paid for) after the termination of the agency, in the following circumstances:

- Where the order had been placed before termination, and the agent would have been entitled to commission had the agency continued.

- Where an order placed within a reasonable period after termination was mainly attributable to the efforts of the agent.

The latter circumstances merit discussion. The purpose is fairly clear: to prevent the agent being deprived of commission for sales achieved by his/her work prior to termination.

The requirement for the order being 'mainly attributable to the agent's efforts' addresses that purpose – it excludes, for instance, an agent claiming commission on sales made purely on the basis that the customer was in the agent's territory. In practice, and as the cases considered in the legal guide below demonstrate, whether particular sales were 'mainly attributable to the agent's efforts' is often a cause for dispute, especially if the product is a complex one and the lead-in time between initial presentation and completed sale is several months or years. The principal might argue that, whilst the initial work was done by the agent, the principal itself (or perhaps a replacement representative) had to do the most important work before and/or after termination to secure the sale. Such arguments are inevitably fact-sensitive.

A more common generic problem arises in this context where the relevant sales are, in effect, re-orders – with nobody exerting any particular 'effort' to achieve them. Agents often claim commission on such sales for a period of, say, 3 or 6 months, on the basis that they originally signed up the customer, so the sales are mainly attributable to them. There is no straightforward answer in such a situation. One might distinguish two kinds of such sales: (1) where particular selling activity has been undertaken by the outgoing agent in respect of a recent product range (a good example would be a new season's range of fashion clothing), and – following termination – customers place further orders for items from that new range; (2) where the principal's product range is relatively stable and customers simply order as and when stocks of particular items are low. In the first situation, the entitlement to pipeline commission would arise; in the second, it would probably not.

Finally, there is the issue of what is a 'reasonable period'. There is no crude yardstick available; it will all depend on the type of product and how it is sold. To take an extreme, real life, scenario: an agent spent several months persuading a buyer at a major UK supermarket to agree to purchase wine from his principal; an agreement was reached in principle for the customer to buy a minimum of so many thousand bottles a year – at which time the principal terminated the agency. Shortly afterwards, the deal was signed for a period of 3 years. In that case, the 'reasonable period' during which the agent was entitled to commission on the relevant sales was properly claimed at 3 years. An agent who promotes a new season's range of clothing or furniture every 6 or 12 months ought to be able to claim in respect of relevant sales up to the end of the ordering season which was in progress when the agency was terminated, but probably no further.

Can the agency contract exclude the right to pipeline commission?

As noted in the legal guide that follows, there is, surprisingly, no clear answer to this yet, though the courts have considered the point, and experts in the field take different views.

Legal advice warning: **If issues arise in relation to a claim for pipeline commission of significant value, it is probably best to seek legal advice.**

Compensation and indemnity

The first question is: which? Normally, this is easy: if there is an election for indemnity in the agency contract, the right is to an indemnity; otherwise, the right is to compensation.

Sometimes, however, the agency contract may be ambiguous; it may even try to give the principal the best of all worlds by providing for the agent to get whichever of the indemnity or compensation is the lesser amount. In those situations, the right is very likely to compensation. However, there may be a dispute. **Legal advice warning: If this issue arises, it is essential to seek legal advice.**

Indemnity

The calculation of an indemnity is, in two respects, rather more precise than the calculation of compensation. First, it is based on actual/prospective sales made by the principal post-termination to specific customers. Secondly, it is capped at the level of one year's average gross commission earnings.

More particularly, the process of calculation is as follows:-

1. Work out the level of business as at the date of termination which has been added by the agent. This includes business done with customers brought by the agent (the agent has to have been instrumental in securing the relationship between principal and customers, but does not have to have been solely responsible for it). It also includes significant increases in the levels of business done with customers who existed when the agency began (or who were introduced without the agent being instrumental during the agency). What is "significant"? There is no clear answer and it may vary from case to case. Adding 100% by value is certainly significant; 50% is probably so (although if that was over a lengthy period, such that the increase in 'real' terms was much less, it might not be); 10% is very likely not; an increase in the range 20-40% might give rise to a dispute depending on the facts.

2. Establish how much of that business the principal was likely (as at the date of termination) to maintain post-termination. It may be all of it; it may be much less, particularly if the agent was going to try to poach the business for a new principal. Extrapolate for a period of years relevant to the agency – for a well-established customer base in a steady market, that might be up to 10 years; for a not very well-established customer base in a volatile and highly competitive market, that might be for only a few years, with a significant presumed drop-off each year.

3. Work out what <u>net</u> commission earnings (i.e. after expenses) the agent would have earned on that business. (Some experts dispute whether it is right to deduct expenses; but that is the law for the moment.)

4. Make any necessary adjustment(s) to ensure the amount would be <u>equitable in the circumstances</u>. *This would rarely apply in practice.* It might include taking account of issues such as: whether the agent has been at fault in failing to perform all his/her duties (though not in circumstances where the entitlement is lost altogether) – that could lead to the amount being reduced; or the agent being subject to a restraint of trade covenant such that s/he could not act for any similar principal for a year post-termination – that could lead to the amount being increased.

5. <u>Apply the cap</u>. This is worked out as the annual average of the last 5 years' gross commission earnings – or the average over the agency if it has been going for a lesser period than 5 years. The amount to be paid will be the sum calculated in steps 1-4 unless that sum exceeds the cap, in which case the capped sum is payable.

Commonly, a relatively stable and successful agency where the agent has introduced a fair amount of business (it does not have to be over a long period) will lead to a calculation which exceeds the cap and therefore the entitlement will be to an amount equivalent to the cap.

However, at the other end of the spectrum – and in marked contrast to the position as regards compensation – if the agent has simply taken over an existing customer base and not introduced any significant new business, then the value of an indemnity will be very low. This is so (however unfair it might seem) even if the agency has been in existence for many years and the product range has altered considerably during that time, such that the agent has had to rely on real effort and talent to maintain the level of sales to those customers. In such a case, the agent could argue that the level of indemnity ought to be adjusted upwards so as to be equitable in all the circumstances; but as yet there is no way of knowing whether and how far such an argument would succeed if the dispute went before a court, as such a scenario has not come before an English court.

A worked example

The agency was for the sale of furniture made in Germany. The product range changed over time. The agency had been running for 7 years. The agent introduced 21 new customers, of whom 15 were still ordering in the final season. There were 30 existing customers when the agent took over, of whom 10 remained at the date of termination. Of those 10, business had only increased over the life of the agency with 2 – in one case by several 100%; in the other by 30%. The principal had been losing business recently to competitors whose products are made in China, overall sales in the relevant territory reducing by about 20% annually over the last couple of years. The agent's expenses were equivalent to about 30% of commission earnings.

For the 15 new customers still ordering, give somewhere between 80—100% of value for the first year; then reduce by 20% (compound) each year for the next about 4 years; after that, it is too uncertain. For the customer with whom business increased by several 100%, give somewhere between 80—100% of the value of the increase for the first year; then reduce by 20% (compound) each year for the next about 4 years. For the customer whose business increased by 30%, there are arguments for including and for excluding: in favour of including is the fact that 30% in a difficult market with a changing product range might be considered significant; in favour of excluding is the fact that in real terms the increase of 30% over 7 years might be equivalent to not much more than 10% after discounting for the relevant rate of inflation.

Calculate the commission the agent would have earned on those sales over that 4-year period, then discount by 30% in respect of expenses.

No need to adjust for equity.

Apply the cap of the average of the last 5 years' actual gross commission earnings, in so far as applicable.

Tip for agents and principals: If the value of the claim is very high, you might want to enlist the assistance of an accounting expert, but in truth the exercise is more a factual and legal one than an accountancy one (by contrast with compensation: see below). If possible, try (generally through legal representatives, but it does not have to be so) to set out your calculation and obtain the same from the other party. That way you can identify where the issues of dispute are and attempt to reach a sensible compromise.

Tip for agents: If the negotiation is happening some time after the termination, ask the principal to provide information as to actual sales to the relevant customers since the agency ended.

Compensation

The calculation of compensation is both easier and much more difficult. It is easier because the yardstick is simply the value of the agency; namely, what the agency is worth to a replacement agent. It is more difficult because the way of measuring/applying that yardstick is, in practice, very unscientific.

The following legal principles must be followed:

- One assesses the value of the agency as at the date of termination; although if there is a dispute as to that value, the court is entitled to take account of actual events post-termination in deciding what was likely to happen as at the date of termination. So if (as sometimes happens) the agent argues that prospects for the agency looked very rosy when it was terminated and the principal argues that turnover was likely to decline, what actually happened might provide an indication of a realistic projection at that time. Although this will only be so if the principal put in place competent alternative sales representation quickly.

- One assumes that the agency would have continued indefinitely for the hypothetical new agent, with the normal cooperation of the principal. In particular, one ignores the fact that the agency could be terminated on relatively short notice; as one ignores the fact that the principal might in theory stop marketing its products for no good reason, etc.

- The value of the agency is **not** dependent on the extent to which the agent has personally built up that value. To take an extreme case, if an agent takes over a valuable agency from a long-standing agent and a month later is run over and dies, the value of the agency is no different to what it was a month earlier when the recent agency commenced.

- By the same token, if the agency was likely to decline post-termination, it does not matter that the reason is nothing to do with the outgoing agent. If, for instance, a principal's products are becoming much less popular or much less competitive, then the agency is clearly of less value.

Multiplicand-multiplier approach

The reason the process of valuation is so imprecise is that commercial agencies do not trade on the open market. So unlike establishing the value of, say, a hairdresser's business (or, for that matter, a house or a motor car), there are no comparable figures a valuer can turn to as a guide.

What tends to happen in practice is that the valuer (usually a chartered accountant) assesses, as at the date of termination, the net income stream (commissions less expenses) for the following year (the 'multiplicand'), and then applies a 'multiplier' to that figure.

The first part of the process is at least fact-based and fairly scientific (though it raises one very controversial issue, which we discuss in a moment).

The second part – selecting the multiplier – is a more subjective and nuanced affair; and it is very common for two valuers (one for the agent and one for the principal) to arrive at very different multipliers for the same agency (unsurprisingly, the one for the agent always being rather higher than the one for the principal). It is not uncommon to read in such an expert valuation report something along the lines: 'I have looked at this or that index of multipliers for businesses in the relevant trade sector and that provides me with a starting point of X; however, this being an agency and not a major company whose shares trade publicly, it is appropriate to apply a discount of Y'. Where X bears no real relationship to the type of business that is a commercial agency; and Y is at best an honest impressionistic attempt to arrive at a sensible value, which cannot be tested objectively.

That said, whilst the analysis is necessarily imprecise and perhaps subjective, the multiplier is intended to reflect the hypothetical purchaser's perception of the risks associated with the agency and, in particular, the risk that the projected income stream would / would not continue, and to that extent, real-world assessments can be made on the facts. The multiplier may be considered as the time which it will take the purchaser to make a profit on its investment. By way of illustration, if the net commissions are £100,000 and the multiplier is 4, the agency is valued at £400,000. Thus it will not be until year 5 that the hypothetical purchaser will see a return on its investment, it taking 4 years to earn back the purchase price. It follows that the higher the multiplier, the greater the prospects are for the agency business viewed from the date of termination.

The calculation is subject to tax payable by the hypothetical purchaser on the future income stream, which can be reflected either at the stage of calculating the net income stream, or by factoring tax in to the multiplier.

Clearly, altering the variables, such as increasing costs (which has the effect of reducing net commissions) or the multiplier, will impact significantly upon the outcome, and these sorts of factors are hotly contested in almost every case.

All this leads to considerable uncertainty, which can only be resolved via commercial negotiation or a Judge or Arbitral Tribunal doing their best to reach a fair result on the evidence before them.

Assessing the net income stream ('multiplicand')

Notional salary

It is noted above that there was one issue which could arise in assessing the net income stream which is particularly controversial – it is this: should a deduction be made for the notional salary of the agent?

So, for example, if the agent used to earn £15,000 p.a. from an agency which took up a quarter of his/her time and on which s/he spent £2,000 p.a. out of pocket, is the net income £13,000, or is it £13,000 less a quarter of the salary for an experienced salesperson in the relevant sector (which may lead to a multiplicand of zero or not much more)?

If the agent is a limited company, this will generally not arise: profits are profits, taking account of all relevant staff costs (though even here if the work is done by one or two owner/director(s), paying themselves by dividends, then the position is not always straightforward). However, if the agent is a natural person, the effect will obviously be considerable.

To deduct for a notional salary in such a situation would appear to be harsh and contrary to the purposes of the Directive. However, it should be noted that the arguments (which differ depending on the facts of each case) continue and there has been no clear, authoritative guidance from the courts.

Tip for agents: If you are thinking of incorporating (for tax reasons, say), bear in mind that you might end up worse off in terms of the level of compensation payable if you have an agency/agencies where the contract does not provide for an indemnity.

Apportionment of expenditure

Another issue which arises very often in assessing the net income stream is how to apportion expenses if the agent has more than one agency (perhaps also acts in other capacities – e.g. as a re-seller).

On one view there is merit in the argument of an agent who says that when the 'leather sofa' agency was terminated, s/he still had to drive round in the same car using the same petrol to the same customers for the other four furniture agencies, so s/he has saved little or no money and therefore there should be little or no deduction for expenses.

On the other hand, pushed to its extreme, this argument would permit an agent to surrender several agencies within a short period (perhaps at the same time) on grounds of retirement or ill health, without making a significant deduction for expenses against the gross income from any of them.

In a high-value case, it might be appropriate to seek a refined apportionment of different categories of expenditure, but the basic rule is: all expenses must be apportioned. So, to take an example, if an agent in the fashion industry pays for show-room space in which items from three of its four agencies are displayed, with one of the three taking up half the space and the other two a quarter each: no deduction should be made in respect of the agency which does not use the show-room; and deductions should be made in respect of the others in the ratio: 2:1:1.

As for the agent who lost the 'leather sofa' agency described above, s/he must give credit for one-fifth of travel expenditure.

Assessing the multiplier

As stated, this is more art than science and all one can really do is to mention some of the factors which tend to have a significant impact (other than the obvious ones of whether the agency was expanding or declining), and to record that – in very broad terms – valuations of agencies that are neither declining rapidly nor growing exponentially tend to come up with multipliers in the range 2-5, with a stable, long-standing agency in the range 3-4 (though higher and lower multipliers may be appropriate and have been applied by the courts).

As to those significant factors:

Factors which would push up the multiplier:-

- product range is well-established with the relevant customer base;
- products are of a type that are not susceptible to trend/fashion;
- principal is market-leader in the relevant products;

- agent unable to compete with ex-principal for a new principal.

Factors which would push down the multiplier:-

- product range not well-established with relevant customer base;
- products are susceptible to fashion/trend (clothes, toys, gift items);
- strong competition from other manufacturers;
- threat of competition of products made more cheaply in other countries (Far East, for example);
- risk of the agent poaching customers for a new principal.

CHAPTER 7B

PAYMENTS FOLLOWING TERMINATION OF THE AGENCY – LEGAL GUIDE

Regulations 8 and 17

What the Regulations and case law say

A key purpose of the Regulations is to protect commercial agents – and nowhere is this more evident than in the entitlements provided for agents at the end of the relationship. Most agents and principals are aware of the fact that on termination an agent will generally be entitled to a lump sum payment, which can be substantial (the circumstances where an agent will not be entitled to such a payment have been discussed above). There is sometimes confusion, however, about the nature of that payment, as the Regulations provide for the payment of compensation *or* an indemnity, and principals and agents often do not know which type of payment is relevant to their situation. This confusion is compounded when it comes to quantifying the agent's entitlements. Whilst the approach in principle to calculating compensation has been set out by the highest court in the land, little is known on the ground about the application of this approach. Further, even now, there has been little by way of guidance from the courts on how the indemnity should be calculated.

As a result, principals and agents often believe at the end of the relationship that the agent is entitled to (something like) a payment of one year's commission calculated as an average of commissions over the preceding years. This is almost always incorrect and the payment is usually: (i) higher, if the payment is compensation based; or (ii) lower if the calculation is on an indemnity basis (though this is not always the case where the agent has added significantly to the ongoing value of the principal's business).

Below, we look at the rules on post-termination payments, which can be found in Regulations 8 and 17. In addition, on termination, an agent may be entitled to payment in lieu of notice (under the contract between the agent and principal and/or under Regulation 15, as discussed in the chapter on termination); and, potentially, damages arising from a principal's breach of Regulation 4 (i.e. the principal's obligation to act dutifully and in good faith).

Commissions on transactions not complete as at termination

It is often the case that, as a result of the efforts of the agent, a principal receives an order from a customer either:

1. Before termination but where the transaction between the principal and customer takes place after termination; or
2. Shortly after termination.

In such circumstances, the agent's contractual right to commission on those transactions may have come to an end – after all, the principal will be getting no benefit until after the agency contract has concluded; and in the absence of an express contractual provision providing for commission on post-termination sales, there may well be no contractual obligation on the principal to make any further payments to the agent.

However, commercial agency has its own rules on commissions that are payable on transactions that are concluded post-termination. Those rules are in Regulation 8, which provides:

> "*Subject to regulation 9 below, a commercial agent shall be entitled to commission on commercial transactions concluded after the agency contract has terminated if—*
>
> "*(a) the transaction is mainly attributable to his efforts during the period covered by the agency contract and if the transaction was entered into within a reasonable period after that contract terminated; or*
>
> "*(b) in accordance with the conditions mentioned in regulation 7 above, the order of the third party reached the principal or the commercial agent before the agency contract terminated.*"

The first question arising from Regulation 8 is: when, for the purposes of Regulation 8, is a transaction "*concluded*". Is it when the order is: (i) placed? (ii) fulfilled? (iii) invoiced? (iv) paid for?

In *Tigana v Decoro*,[85] the court held that in the circumstances of that case a transaction was "*concluded*", for the purposes of Regulation 8, when the order was placed (and, presumably, accepted), though little explanation for that conclusion is given. A possible explanation for such a conclusion is that the contract for sale between principal and customer is made when the order is placed and accepted, and therefore that is when one would expect the transaction to be "*concluded*" for the purposes of Regulation 8. However, that interpretation of "*concluded*" is difficult to reconcile with the wording of Regulation 8. This is because the introductory words to Regulation 8 make it clear that a commercial agent is entitled to commission on "*transactions concluded after the agency contract has terminated*", where, according to 8(b), the order reached the principal <u>before</u> termination. The transaction cannot be concluded both before and after termination. In any event, such an approach to the word "*concluded*" in Regulation 8 is favourable to the agent, as it comes early in the sales process (i.e. it is not dependent on payment). However, in light of Regulation 11, if the customer subsequently does not pay the principal for a reason for which the principal is not to blame, then there will be no entitlement to commission in respect of such an order.

Orders already received

We deal with commissions on orders received before termination first as this is the simplest element of Regulation 8. The Regulation is simple – if the customer's order is received by the principal before termination, even if they are not fulfilled until after termination, the agent is entitled to commission.

85 [2003] EWHC 23 (QB) at [54].

Orders that are mainly attributable to the agent and received within reasonable period of termination

This limb of Regulation 8 provides for an agent to receive commission on orders placed by customers after termination where the sale is:

1. "*Mainly attributable*" to the agent's efforts during the life of the agency contract; and

2. Entered into within a reasonable period after the termination of the agency contract.

What the Regulations do not explain is what "*mainly attributable*" means, and what a "*reasonable period*" is. Below we explain how these tests have been applied by the courts.

"Mainly attributable" and "Reasonable period"

There are circumstances where it would be obvious that a post-termination order is mainly attributable to an agent's efforts, and that it took place within a reasonable period of termination. Take a fashion collection that has a six-month life span. A customer may order 100 dresses as a result of an agent's efforts before termination. After those orders are placed and the agent's commission paid, the principal may terminate the agency contract. In the meantime, the dresses sell well and three months after the initial order (and two months after termination), the customer orders 100 more dresses from the collection that had initially been shown by the agent. The agent is no longer under contract, but clearly the customer is placing further orders on the basis of the agent's initial efforts. In such circumstances, the agent would be able to bring a claim for commissions on the second order under Regulation 8 as:

1. The order would be attributable to the agent's efforts pre-termination; and

2. Given the nature of the market and the goods, the transaction did occur within a reasonable period.

By the same reasoning, if an agent is engaged to sell high-cost, complex industrial equipment, the process of making a sale may take many months' or even years' work, and the agent may put in this groundwork but have its contract terminated before the customer's procurement process is complete. If, following termination, an order is placed, provided that the principal has not stepped in and undertaken most or all of the key work to secure the sale, the agent is likely to have a good claim to Regulation 8 commission. In these circumstances, such a Regulation 8 claim is likely to be valuable (as was the case in *PJ Pipe & Valve v Audco India*[86]).

In many markets and in respect of many goods, however, determining whether a sale is mainly attributable to an agent, and assessing whether the sale took place within a reasonable period, is not straightforward. Take, for example, confectionery. A customer may purchase branded confectionery via an agent for many years. However, that customer may have purchased the goods in any event and indeed, is likely to continue to purchase them whether or not an agent is involved in the process and regardless of whether another agent is appointed. In these circumstances, the assessment of the value of the Regulation 8 payment becomes less certain. The agent may have, in the early days, brought the customer to the principal, but by the time of termination, may have little causal effect in the sales process. In these circumstances, an agent may have difficulty showing that post termination sales were mainly attributable to its efforts and also in showing that the reasonable period has any significant length (these are fast moving goods with a high stock turnover). It must not be forgotten that Regulation 17 provides effective compensation for the agent's introduction of customers per se. The agent will therefore have to show something more done by it in respect of the specific sales in dispute to justify an entitlement to commission under Regulation 8(a). A close analysis of the facts of each case will therefore need to be undertaken, as the court recognised in *Tigana v Decoro*,[87] in which the court said: "*the Regulation designedly confers a degree of flexibility available to each case under consideration, for example, a "reasonable period" in one case will not be in another case*".

86 [2005] EWHC 1904 (QB)

87 [2003] EWHC 23 (QB) at para 55

The court, in the case of *PJ Pipe & Valve v Audco India,*[88] concluded that the test under Regulation 8 as to whether a sale completed post-termination was "*mainly attributable*" to a commercial agent was similar to the common law test; that is, one should assess whether the agent was the "*effective cause*" of the transaction. The court noted that whilst there may be other causes relating to the transaction, an agent will be entitled to commission if its activities were the effective cause. The court reached a similar conclusion in *Tigana v Decoro*,[89] in which the Judge said: "*it is also clear that the phrase "mainly attributable" connotes a causative link between the efforts of the commercial agent and the conclusion of the transaction (albeit after the agency contract has terminated). One might perhaps see an analogy with the familiar English Legal phase "effective cause""*.

In *Tigana v Decoro* the court noted that in determining whether a transaction is mainly attributable to an agent, and whether it occurred within a reasonable period, the "*overall task... is one of judgment and assessment... by reference to the facts of the case.*" It also highlighted the difficulty with applying principles from the cases on this issue to other circumstances, noting that "*Everything...will depend upon the circumstances of each case*".

Following an analysis of the facts of the case, in *Tigana*, the Judge concluded that whilst the agent's activities were "*front loaded*" (i.e. his primary role had been to introduce new customers to the principal at the outset of the agency), an important part of his role was to maintain regular liaison with customers and to secure repeat orders; as a result, post-termination orders were mainly attributable to him for a period of 9 months (which was the period before he was fully replaced with alternative representation). This resulted in a Regulation 8(a) payment of $606,836.64.

In *Ingmar GB Ltd v. Eaton Leonard Ltd,*[90] the Judge held that "*although the transaction was entered into 21 months after the agency was terminated it was "within a reasonable period" having regard to the nature of the agency, the product and the customer base.*" In that case, the principal manufac-

---

88 [2005] EWHC 1904 (QB)

89[2003] EWHC 23 (QB) at para 55

90 [2003] EWHC 23 (QB) at para 54;

tured and sold sophisticated tube and pipe bending machines and associated equipment mainly designed for the aircraft and automotive industries.

In *McQuillan v McCormick*,[91] the Judge took a very light-touch approach to valuing the Regulation 8 claim. After determining when the assessment should run from, the Judge said: "*This is a difficult exercise but I propose to value it* [i.e. the Regulation 8 claim] *on the basis of 2 months' commission...*" There is no explanation in the written version of the judgment as to how the Judge concluded that two months was a reasonable period, and no discussion as to whether the sales made in the two months following termination were mainly attributable to the agent (in contrast to the detailed analysis of the facts in *Tigana*). This may be because it was not argued by the parties, and they may have accepted that all sales made in the two months following termination were mainly attributable to the agent. That said, the sum awarded by the Judge in respect of Regulation 8 was almost £30,000, so it is surprising, given that a longer period may have produced a significantly higher payment, that there is not greater discussion of this point in the judgment.

Can the agency contract override Regulation 8?

Agency contracts may contain clauses to the effect that an agent will not be entitled to any commission on any orders received by the principal following termination (even if the order occurs within a reasonable period following termination and the order is mainly attributable to the agent). That clearly contradicts Regulation 8, so the question is: are the parties allowed, in their contract, to exclude the operation of Regulation 8?

The matter has not been decided definitively by the English courts (though it has been considered by them) and therefore, where a contract does contain what might be read as a derogation from Regulation 8, this is a hotly contested issue.

91 [2010] EWHC 1112 (QB)

The Regulations do contain some non-derogation provisions. For example, Regulation 19 provides that the parties cannot agree to disapply Regulation 17. This means a term in a contract between a principal and agent that provides that the agent is not entitled to a Regulation 17 payment on termination is null and void.

There is no such (express) provision in respect of Regulation 8. On the face of it, this would appear to evidence the fact that when the Directive (and the Regulations implementing them) were being drafted, the drafters considered whether or not the parties to a contract of commercial agency would be able to derogate from a particular provision and made it clear when they could not (and therefore, by omission, when they could). It appears that the conclusion reached was that the parties should be free to choose whether to derogate from Regulation 8 or not.

There is a further factor supporting this conclusion. A draft of the Directive which gave rise to the Regulations stated that parties could not derogate from Regulation 8, whereas this provision was not included within the final version. It is, therefore, arguable that the legislature had considered whether the parties to a contract of commercial agency should be free to contract out of Regulation 8, initially taking the view that they should not be able to do so, but later concluded that they could, should they choose to do so.

The approach of the European Court of Justice (as it then was) in the case of *Volvo Car Germany GmbH v Autohof Weidensdorf GmbH*[92] supports this type of analysis. In that case, the ECJ considered the inference that ought to be drawn where there was wording in a draft of the Directive that was removed from the final version. It was of the view that if wording that had been in a draft was removed from the final version, that wording was intended not to apply. Whilst that case focussed on the indemnity provisions contained within the Regulations, by analogy it is arguable that the court would find that the removal of the non-derogation provisions from Article 8 from the draft of the Directive meant that the legislature had intended that the parties could contract out of it.

92 Case C-203/09

Morland J agreed with that analysis in *Ingmar GB Ltd v. Eaton Leonard Ltd*,[93] when he said: "*It should be noted that there is no non-derogation article equivalent to Article 19 applicable to Articles 7 and 8. In my judgment the absence of such a specific non-derogation article means that commercial agents and principals may derogate contractually from articles 7 and 8 but only so far as they do not thwart the purpose of the Council Directive.*"

Whilst this statement supports the pro-derogation argument, it is *obiter*, and therefore not binding on other courts. In addition, the caveat "*but only so far as they do not thwart the purpose of the Council Directive*" is grist to the mill of those who will argue that derogation is prohibited. They will say, with some force, that: (i) the key purpose of the Directive is to protect commercial agents (which is unarguable); (ii) principals have greater bargaining power and can force agents to accept unfavourable contractual terms (again this is generally true); (iii) a provision derogating from Regulation 8 is to the detriment of the agent; and as a result (iv) a derogation provision thwarts the purpose of the Directive. In any event, such considerations certainly support the proposition that for a contractual provision to constitute a lawful derogation from the entitlements in Regulation 8, it must be worded in sufficiently clear terms to that effect.

The waters are further muddied by Regulation 11, which provides:

> "*11.— Extinction of right to commission*
>
> *(1) The right to commission can be extinguished only if and to the extent that—*
>
> *(a) it is established that the contract between the third party and the principal will not be executed; and*
>
> *(b) that fact is due to a reason for which the principal is not to blame.*
>
> *(2) Any commission which the commercial agent has already received shall be refunded if the right to it is extinguished.*

93 [2001] EWHC 3 (QB);

> *(3) Any agreement to derogate from paragraph (1) above to the detriment of the commercial agent shall be void."*

Regulation 8 is quite clearly a "*right to commission*"; it states that the agent "*shall be entitled to commission*" on post-termination transactions in the circumstances set out in Regulation 8. Therefore, is Regulation 11(3) an indirect non-derogation provision? It is certainly arguable that this is so, given that Regulation 11 sets out the circumstances when the right to commission can be extinguished and (like Regulation 19) states that the provisions of Regulation 11 cannot be derogated from to the agent's detriment.

In *Software Incubator Ltd v Computer Associates UK Ltd,*[94] the court held that by their contract, the parties did exclude Regulation 8 and there had been a valid exclusion of the agent's Regulation 8 claim. It is not clear if any of the above arguments were made in that case as the judgment does not contain an analysis of these points. Of note, however, is that whilst the court found that the agent was not entitled to commissions on post-termination transactions under Regulation 8, it held that the agent was entitled under the common law to the same commission on deals which emerged after termination but whose effective cause was the agent while the agency was on foot, on the basis that the agreement either impliedly or expressly contained a right to such commissions.

Contracts by which the parties appear to derogate from Regulation 8 are prevalent, and principals can take comfort from the fact that there is a good case to be made that the Regulation is capable of exclusion. However, as this matter has not been definitively decided, and as a key purpose of the Regulations is to protect agents, agents will continue to argue (with some justification) that Regulation 8 cannot be excluded. Until the matter is decided authoritatively by the courts, it will remain one of the factors that principals, agents and their advisers will weigh in the balance when formulating, prosecuting, defending and negotiating the settlement of, claims.

94 [2016] EWHC 1587 (QB)

Termination payments: Indemnity or compensation? What if the agency contract is silent or ambiguous?

Under the Regulations, upon termination of the agency contract, a commercial agent falling within the definition in Regulation 2 is, subject to Regulation 18(a) (i.e. the termination is justified because of the agent's breach), entitled to a post-termination payment. By virtue of Regulation 19, the parties may not derogate from regulations 17 and 18 to the detriment of the commercial agent before the agency contract expires.

Regulation 17(2) provides that except where the agency contract provides otherwise, the agent will be entitled to be compensated rather than indemnified.

This means that if the agent is to be paid an indemnity, the contact must say so. Otherwise, compensation will be payable.

The key difference between an indemnity and compensation is that an indemnity is limited to the lower of either:

1. the amount determined in a manner likely to be in accordance with the approach detailed below; or

2. one year's commission calculated from the agent's average annual remuneration over the preceding five years and if the contract goes back less than 5 years, over the relevant period (essentially a cap).

As a result, if the contract provides for an indemnity, a principal will know before it terminates the agency contract what its maximum liability will be under Regulation 17.

On the other hand, compensation is unlimited and the quantum of the compensation payment cannot be predicted with certainty as it will be determined by a Judge with the benefit of expert evidence from forensic accountants instructed by the parties.

As a general rule, except where the agent earns relatively modest commissions, compensation payments are higher than indemnity payments.

What happens when a contract between the agent and principal provides that the agent is entitled, on termination, to an indemnity or compensation, whichever is the lower? That was the question in *Shearman (t/a Charles Shearman Agencies) v Hunter Boot Ltd*,[95] where the contract provided that:

> "*The Agent will not be entitled to the indemnity referred to in clause 14.4 but will be entitled to compensation for the damage it suffers as a result of the termination of its relations with the Agent if the amount of such compensation would be less than the amount payable by way of indemnity*".

Surprisingly, given that one of the purposes of the Regulations is to protect agents against the bargaining power of the principal, and the courts' long history of applying the Regulations so as to give effect to that purpose, shortly before the trial of the claim, the principal (Hunter, the manufacturer of wellington boots) applied for summary judgment claiming that any entitlement that the agent (Mr Shearman) had under Regulation 17 was to an indemnity and not to compensation. This mattered because Mr Shearman claimed that compensation would amount to "*a sum not less than £1,454,400.'* However, an indemnity would be capped at an amount equivalent to Mr Shearman's average annual commission income over the last five years of his agency which Hunter claimed would be no more than £204,000.

In that case, the Judge held that whilst the parties were free to choose contractual terms, it was necessary to give effect to the purpose of the Regulations; that is, to protect commercial agents. The clause in question sought to give the agent the worst possible outcome on termination; something that the court found (unsurprisingly) was not consistent with the Regulations. As a result, the entire clause fell away so that the agent was entitled to compensation.

Clearly, a choice needs to be made at the outset; the court will not allow a principal to hedge its bets.

95 [2014] EWHC 47 (QB)

However, in a later case, *Brand Studio Ltd v St John Knits Inc,*[96] the court reached a different conclusion in respect of a similar but differently worded clause in the contract, on the basis that the parties had opted for an indemnity and then the principal had unlawfully added an additional provision to the effect that compensation would be payable if that were lower – which, the court found, meant that the offending additional provision could be 'severed' (in effect, crossed out). Permission was given to appeal that decision, but the case settled before the appeal was heard.

Effect of principal discovering agent's wrongdoing after giving notice to terminate/after termination

The basic position, as set out in the earlier chapter on termination, is that if an agent is in fundamental breach of the agency contract, and the principal terminates because of that breach, the principal may be able to avoid paying an indemnity or compensation under Regulation 18(a). However, to rely on Regulation 18(a), the termination must be because of that breach.[97]

This means, as noted in the chapter on termination, that if a principal terminates without any particular reason (for example, it simply wishes to take the sales role in-house), and finds out following termination that the agent was in breach of the agreement before termination such that the principal could have terminated as a result of that breach, without liability, the principal cannot retrospectively use that breach to avoid liability.

Whilst the interpretation given by the courts to the wording of Regulation 18(a) is, on a literal basis, unarguable, the result could be harsh on a principal as a disloyal fraudulent agent of whose nefarious activities the principal was unaware would remain entitled to a post-termination payment.

The courts have spotted this potential injustice and, in respect of indemnities, have addressed this issue. As has been seen, an agent is only entitled

96 [2015] EWHC 3143 (QB), [2016] 1 Lloyd's Rep 179

97 *Volvo Car Germany GmbH v Autohof Weidensdorf GmbH* (case C-203/09) – as discussed in the termination chapter above

to an indemnity if payment is "*equitable having regard to all the circumstances*".[98] In the case of *Volvo Car Germany GmbH v Autohof Weidensdorf GmbH*,[99] ECJ held that:

> "...*a commercial agent is to be entitled to an indemnity if and to the extent that the payment of that indemnity is equitable having regard to all the circumstances. The possibility cannot, therefore, be ruled out that the agent's conduct may be taken into account in the assessment made to determine the fairness of his indemnity.*"

This leaves scope to argue that the amount of the indemnity should be reduced, or extinguished, in circumstances where it would not be equitable to make the payment. Any wrongful conduct by the agent would therefore clearly be a factor to be weighed in the balance, even if that conduct was not the reason for the termination.

Whilst the courts have dealt with this issue in relation to indemnities, there is no equivalent binding case law in relation to compensation. Further, under the Regulations, there is no requirement for the compensation payment to be made only if it is equitable to do so, and so the *Volvo* case cannot be read as applying to compensation too.

However, there may yet be a route for a principal to avoid paying compensation to an agent when the principal discovers its agent's breaches of contract only after termination, and this has been considered (on an *obiter*, and therefore non-binding basis) by the Court of Appeal.

The starting point for this analysis is the Regulations. Under Regulation 17(6), the agent is compensated for "*the damage he suffers as a result of the termination of his relations with his principal*", and it is the "*damage suffered*" formulation that may hold the key.

In *Cooper v Pure Fishing (UK) Limited*,[100] Lord Justice Tuckey, giving the leading Judgment in the Court of Appeal, stated:

---

98 Regulation 17(3)(b)

99 Case C-203/09

100 [2004] EWCA Civ 375

> *"In a case where it was subsequently discovered that the agent had been guilty of fraud which would have justified immediate termination, it could probably be argued that he has suffered no damage as a result of the termination".*

The "*damage*" that an agent suffers as a result of termination of the agency agreement is that they are denied the right to earn future commission from the sale of their principal's products. In the case where the agent was in fundamental breach of the agency contract before termination, such that had the principal been aware of the breaches it would have terminated the agency contract, it is arguable that the agent did not suffer "*damage*" within the meaning of Regulation 17(6) when the agency contract ultimately ended, as the contract was terminable without a Regulation 17 liability by the principal.

In addition, it is arguable that the case of *Cureton v Mark Insulations Limited*[101] means that any compensation an agent would be entitled to on termination could be reduced where it was discovered after termination that the agent had been in fundamental breach of contract before termination. In *Cureton*, where an agent's alleged fraud was considered, Mr Justice Bean said:

> *"I heard interesting submissions from Counsel on the applicability of the doctrine of Boston Deep Sea Fishing Limited v Ansell to this case, the question being whether fraud of a commercial agent discovered subsequent to summary termination of an agency agreement on other grounds defeats any claim for damages for wrongful termination of the agreement...*
>
> *"Mr Benzie* [of Counsel] *was disposed to concede that is does, and I agree."*

The detail of the submissions which gave rise to this conclusion is not set out in the report of that case; however, it lends weight to a principal's argument should such a scenario arise.

101 [2006] EWHL 2279 (QB)

However, both these cases must be treated with caution on this point, since they were decided before *Lonsdale* (see below) and therefore did not take into account the House of Lords' analysis of the entitlement to compensation set out in that case – which, arguably, is not susceptible to reduction by reason of later discovered misconduct, since that misconduct (depending on its nature) may not affect the 'value of the agency' which *Lonsdale* established as the basis of the quantification of compensation.

The relevance of sub-agents

The position of sub-agents under the Regulations is considered earlier. As noted, in *Light v Ty Europe,*[102] the Court of Appeal found that sub-agents were not the principal's commercial agents within the meaning of the Regulations, and therefore were not protected by the Regulations.

However, the court suggested that the sub-agents may still be entitled to a share of the managing agent's post-termination payment, presumably on the basis that (i) the payment is recognition of the goodwill generated with customer, (ii) that it is the sub-agents who are generating that goodwill, and (iii) that it would be unjust for the managing agent to be compensated for the damage suffered on termination but for the sub-agents not to be.

In this respect, in *Light v Ty*, the court said that it could see no reason why as the managing agent's agents the sub-agents should not have been able to establish a stake in the managing agent's compensation claim.

But the court added: "*Whether they could have compelled SCS* [the managing agent] *to make such a claim is more problematical, but a combination of commercial pressure and resourceful lawyers might have done the trick.*"

What that commercial pressure could be, and how those "*resourceful lawyers*" could do the trick, depends on the facts of any particular case. One route for the lawyers to consider may be via the implication of terms into the contract between the managing and sub-agents, such that, for example, the sub-agent would be entitled to a share in any post-termination payments the managing agent obtained from the principal, and that the

102 [2003] EWCA Civ 1238

managing agent must exercise its rights vis-à-vis the principal in the sub-agents' best interests. Such arguments would not be straightforward however and the courts will not lightly imply terms into contracts.[103] Again, it should be noted that this case was decided before *Lonsdale* and the remarks quoted above could be considered not to be consistent with the analysis in *Lonsdale*.

How to calculate compensation

Lonsdale

Where an agency contract does not provide for an indemnity payment on termination, an agent can claim compensation under Regulation 17(6), which entitles a commercial agent to compensation for the damage suffered as a result of the termination of relations with its principal.

Such a claim would be valued by the court applying the principals set out by the House of Lords in *Lonsdale (t/a Lonsdale Agencies) v Howard & Hallam Limited*[104] and in this respect the court will be assisted by expert evidence from forensic accountants instructed by the parties.

Before *Lonsdale* in 2007, there was considerable uncertainty as to how compensation payments under the Regulations should be calculated. *Lonsdale* resolved most of that uncertainty by laying out the principles that should underpin the calculation.

The claimant in Lonsdale was a commercial agent for a shoe manufacturer. In 2003 the principal, whose business was in decline, ceased trading and terminated the agent's contract. The agent sought compensation under Regulation 17(6), and whilst his entitlement to compensation was accepted, the amount was disputed. The principal paid him £7,500 but the agent brought proceedings claiming £19,670, the equivalent of two years' gross commission averaged over the last five years of his agency (which was the French approach to calculating compensation), less the amount already received. In 1997 to 1998 his gross annual commission had been almost £17,000, but by 2002 to 2003 it had fallen to £9,621.

---

103 *Marks & Spencer plc v BNP Paribas Securities Services Trust Company (Jersey) Ltd* [2015] UKSC 72; a term will only be implied if, without the term, the contract would lack commercial or practical coherence (at [21])

104 [2007] UKHL 32

The judge at first instance, taking into account that at the date of termination of the agency the principal's business had been in serious decline, awarded the agent £5,000. The agent appealed to the Court of Appeal, and when the Court of Appeal rejected that appeal, he appealed to the House of Lords.

The House of Lords dismissed the appeal, and held that:

1. The compensation payable under regulation 17(6) of the Regulations was to be calculated by reference to the value of the agency on the assumption that it had continued;
2. There was no reason to follow the French method of calculation as:
    a. Calculation of the compensation payment was a matter for each member state to decide and there was no reason to adopt the French practice of valuing agencies at twice gross annual commission;
    b. Commercial agencies in France operated in market conditions different from those prevailing in England; and
    c. Taking an approach different from the French would not fail to properly implement the Directive.
3. The value of an agency depended on the circumstances actually existing at the time of termination, in particular what its earning prospects had been and what people would have been prepared to pay for it; and
4. The judge had been entitled to conclude that, since the claimant's agency had been producing a modest and falling income in a steadily deteriorating environment and there was no evidence that anyone would have paid anything for it, £5,000 compensation was adequate.

Giving the leading Judgment, Lord Hoffman summarised the approach as follows (a critical part of the reasoning is underlined):

> *"[12] Like any other exercise in valuation, this requires one to say what could reasonably have been obtained, at the date of termination, for the rights which the agent had been enjoying. For this purpose it is obviously necessary to assume that the agency would have continued and the hypothetical purchaser would have been able properly to perform the agency contract. He must be assumed to have been able to take over the agency and (if I may be allowed the metaphor) stand in the shoes of the agent, even if, as a matter of contract, the agency was not assignable or there were in practice no dealings in such agencies... What has to be valued is the income stream which the agency would have generated.*
>
> *"[13] On the other hand, as at present advised, I see no reason to make any other assumptions contrary to what was the position in the real world at the date of termination. As one is placing a present value upon future income, one must discount future earnings by an appropriate rate of interest. If the agency was by its terms or in fact unassignable, it must be assumed, as I have said, that the hypothetical purchaser would have been entitled to take it over. But there is no basis for assuming that he would then have obtained an assignable asset...*
>
> *"Likewise, if the market for the products in which the agent dealt was rising or declining, this would have affected what a hypothetical purchaser would have been willing to give. He would have paid fewer years' purchase for a declining agency than for one in an expanding market.*
>
> *"If the agent would have had to incur expense or do work in earning his commission, it cannot be assumed that the hypothetical purchaser would have earned it gross or without having to do anything."*

It is often the case that, whilst principals and agents agree that the agent is entitled to compensation, valuation of that compensation is a major battleground, as whilst the principles of calculation are clear, the application of those to the facts is often disputed.

An interesting approach was taken by the principal in *Warren v Drukkerij Flach B.V.*[105] In that case, the agent retired. Within 6 months of his retirement, £230,000 of orders were placed with the principal by two of the agent's customers. The agent brought a claim for compensation against the principal under the Regulations.

The principal sought to defend the claim by arguing that no compensation would be payable because the agency had no value. The evidence upon which the principal relied was that:

1. there was in fact no corporeal buyer who would be prepared to pay anything for the agency; and
2. the principal and customer were dealing directly with each other at the end of the agency and did not wish to continue dealing through an agent.

Given Lord Hoffman's use of the phrase "*hypothetical purchaser*" in *Lonsdale*, it is surprising that the principal argued that compensation would not be payable because there was no actual purchaser prepared to buy the agency. It is perhaps not surprising that the court rejected that argument, holding that not finding an actual identifiable purchaser did not mean the agency had no value. It is always to be assumed that there is a hypothetical purchaser for the agency at the date of termination. The question is what (if anything) the hypothetical purchaser would pay. Further, the evidence in relation to the principal's direct contact with its customers was not compelling. As a result, the court held that the principal had failed in the "*formidable task*" of establishing that the agency had no value and upheld the agent's award of compensation.

Whilst the court in *Warren v Drukkerij Flach B.V.* said that it is a "*formidable task*" to establish that an agency had no value, there will be circumstances in which an agency will be deemed valueless.

In *Lonsdale*, the court considered the Scottish case of *King v Tunnock Ltd.*[106] In that case, the relevant part of the principal's business had closed

105 [2014] EWCA Civ 993

106 2000 SC 424

and in the light of that, the court in *Lonsdale* said that "*no one would have given anything for the right to earn future commissions on the sale of the products where there were none to be sold*".

The court in *Lonsdale* also found that if commissions were very low, and took a great deal of work to earn, an agency would be valueless. The court held that "*it is hard to see why anyone should have paid for the privilege of a full time job which earned him* [i.e. the agent] *less than he would have been paid as a bus conductor*".

It should also be noted that an argument will arise as to whether the Regulation 17 payment should be reduced to take account of the payment made under Regulation 8. This issue was considered in *The Software Incubator Limited v Computer Associates UK Limited,*[107] where the court concluded that a Regulation 8 payment may reduce the Regulation 17 payment. The court said:

> "*[180] A question arises as to whether credit should be given in the Regulation 17 award for any award under Regulation 8. Intuitively, one might think it should since in both awards, the actual estimated further income streams are taken into account. However, one award is based on a valuation representing the "statutory" award and the other is a defined right akin to clauses in relation to future sales that one might normally see in agency contracts anyway. In McQuillan it is true that HHJ Behrens said that credit would have to be given in respect of the Regulation 8 award but that was in the context of a contractual claim not the Regulation 17 claim – see paragraph 171 of his judgment.*
>
> "*[181] … he* [the valuation expert] *suggested there that commission payable under Regulation 8 may have an impact on the question of compensation under Regulation 17 because the hypothetical purchaser would not receive that particular pipeline commission – so this fact could lead to a reduction in the valuation. … I think there is something in what he said because the removal of a pipeline commission might affect the value given to the agency as a whole. However it is a question in each case whether it would. The difference may be*

107 [2016] EWHC 1587 (QB)

> *de minimis, for example when one compares the award under Regulation 8 and the size of the valuation. That, I believe, is the case here. I do not believe that the modest Regulation award here would affect the notional value placed on the agency and indeed there is no real evidence to the contrary, as a matter of valuation. Accordingly, I give no credit against the Regulation 17 award because of the Regulation 8 award.*"

In the *Software Incubator* case, the Regulation 8 commission totalled less than £10,000 and was therefore de minimis in respect of the Regulation 17 compensation.

In *Monk v Largo Foods Ltd*,[108] the Court considered the treatment of this issue in the *Software Incubator* case and did reduce the Regulation 17 payment because of the Regulation 8 payment. Whilst making it clear that this issue will depend on the facts of each case, the Court said:

> "*Approached from first principles, a potential purchaser acquiring the agency would be acquiring an income-stream from the date of purchase. To the extent that any significant part of that income stream in the first year would be payable to the seller and not to the purchaser, I would expect the purchaser to allow for that in the purchase price. In this case, the Regulation 8 sales to Tesco in Great Britain formed a major part of the agency, with sales to Tesco being a significant part of the sales pipeline which any hypothetical purchaser would be acquiring. The fact that commission of £74,280 on those sales would go to Mr Monk would clearly impact the amount a hypothetical purchaser would pay for the agency to some degree. However, I do not accept that a "pound for pound" reduction is appropriate. I believe a reduction of about half the amount – £37,000 – would fairly reflect the fact that a significant part of the commission in the first year of any purchase would have been payable to Mr Monk under Regulation 8.*"

108 [2016] EWHC 1837 (Comm)

Valuation of Regulation 17 compensation payments

As noted above, the calculation is undertaken by the court generally by reference to expert forensic accountancy evidence.

As is clear under *Lonsdale*, when valuing the compensation claim "*what has to be valued is the income stream which the agency would have generated.*" In effect, this requires a valuation of the agency business on the basis that a hypothetical seller and hypothetical purchaser were valuing it for sale and purchase at the date of termination.

At paragraph 28 of *Lonsdale*, Lord Hoffmann said: "*What it* [the agency] *would fetch depends upon circumstances as they existed in the real world at the time: what the earnings prospects of the agency were and what people would have been willing to pay for similar businesses at the time.*"

The most common method of calculation is the capitalised earnings basis, where the valuation is determined by multiplying the net earnings of the business by a suitable price-earnings ratio. This methodology is generally most appropriate for mature businesses with steady income streams.[109] A practical guide to how this calculation is effected in practice is set out in Chapter 7A.

As explained in the practical guide, the first part of the calculation leads to the valuer/court arriving at an annual net sum which they consider the hypothetical purchaser of the agency would receive in commissions in the year following termination (the multiplicand).

The court will then apply a multiplier to arrive at a valuation for the agency business being purchased by the hypothetical purchaser and in so doing the court will be assisted by expert evidence from forensic accountants, who will themselves often rely on published indices[110]. Whilst it is possible to review the cases to see what multipliers the courts have ap-

---

109 A discounted cashflow ("DCF") calculation may, in some circumstances, be appropriate, but this method is less common in commercial agency cases. In the DCF method, the valuation is determined based on the present value of future cash flows anticipated to be generated by the business.

110 For example, the PERDa private company valuation database, the BDO private company price index, the Small and Medium Enterprises Valuation Index published by the UK200 Group.

plied, as each multiplier is fact-specific, findings in the cases do not directly read across. This was noted by Popplewell J in *W Nagel (a firm) v Pluczenik Diamond Company NV,*[111] in which he said:

> "[*114] I should record that* [one of the experts] *referred to multipliers used in other cases, in particular Berry v Laytons [2009] EWHC 1591 (QB): pre-tax multiplier of 4, equivalent to post-tax multiplier of c. 5.5; Invicta v International Brands Ltd [2013] EWHC 1564 (QB): post-tax multiplier of 4.5; Alan Ramsay Sales & marketing Ltd v Typhoo Tea Ltd [2016] EWHC 486 (Comm): post-tax multiplier of 4; Monk & Collins v Largo Foods Ltd [2016] EWHC 1837 (Comm): post-tax multiplier of 4. He was right, however, to treat these as of no real assistance because they concern different agencies and each case is highly fact specific.*"

It should be noted that the valuation is undertaken, hypothetically, at the date of termination, and requires an assessment at that date of the prospects of the agency. By the time of trial, significant time is likely to have passed since termination and what actually happened to the market and the agency will be known. In *Lonsdale* Lord Hoffman was alive to this issue and he said:

> "[39] *What matters, of course, is what would have appeared likely at the date of termination and not what actually happened afterwards. But I do not think that the court is required to shut its eyes to what actually happened. It may provide evidence of what the parties were likely to have expected to happen.*"

The court will therefore be able to sense check the hypothetical date of termination assessment by reference to what really happened after that date. However, there will be cases where a sensible calculation at the date of termination turns out to be confounded by unpredicted subsequent event(s). In that situation, it is the termination-date calculation which applies – which can work very much to the advantage of one or the other party.

111 [2017] EWHC 1750 (Comm)

An issue that has been considered frequently by the courts is the relevance to the calculation of the Regulation 17 compensation of the principal's ability to terminate the agency in accordance with the terms of the contract. In theory, if the agent's contract can be terminated, then the price a hypothetical purchaser would be willing to pay would be reduced to reflect the risk of termination.

In *Alan Ramsay Sales & Marketing Ltd v Typhoo Tea Ltd,*[112] the court held that the ability of the principal to terminate was irrelevant to the calculation of the Regulation 17 compensation. Flaux J said:

> "*[100] In his submissions, Mr Thomas QC [for the defendant] placed great emphasis on this point, saying that, in the real world, any valuation would take account of the fact that the agency was terminable after twelve months. However, I agree with Mr Segal QC that this is a heterodox approach. As is clear from [12] of Lord Hoffmann's judgment in Lonsdale quoted above: 'it is obviously necessary to assume that the agency would have continued and the hypothetical purchaser would have been able properly to perform the agency contract', in other words the valuation for the purpose of the Regulation is on the basis that the agency continues, with the purchaser performing the agency agreement in accordance with its terms, and the principal not invoking any termination or notice provision. Even if this point were not absolutely clear from Lonsdale, what is essentially the same argument was rejected by the Court of Appeal in an earlier case on the Regulations, Page v Combined Shipping & Trading [1997] 3 All ER 656: see per Staughton LJ at 660d-h. Accordingly, in my judgment, the notice period is to be disregarded in valuing the agency and the assumption should be made that, in the absence of external evidence of matters, such as financial difficulty or a trade in terminal decline, the agency would have continued.*"

However, the High Court has not been entirely consistent on this point. In *The Software Incubator Ltd v Computer Associates UK Ltd,*[113] the court

112 [2016] EWHC 486 (Comm), [2016] 4 W.L.R. 59

113 [2016] EWHC 1587 (QB)

said that the right of termination can be factored into the calculation of the Regulation 17 compensation:

> "*[165]. [A]s a matter of law, it is said that no account can be taken of the fact that at some point in the future, the Agreement might be terminated either by CA or indeed by the agent—in the latter case, of course, no right to a Regulation 17 award would arise. I accept that one cannot say that any valuer must proceed on the basis that the principal for example will take immediate steps itself to terminate at the first available opportunity here on 3 months' notice. But nor do I accept the converse which is that the valuer cannot take into account the prospect of a lawful termination on notice at some point in the future. Otherwise, subject only to any shelf-life of the product any notional valuation would have to assume that the agency would last forever. I do not believe that this is realistic…*
>
> "*[167] …it seems to me that in the real world some account has to be taken of the prospect of the agency terminating especially where it is not a fixed term agreement.*
>
> *[168] And in practice, a standard net earnings valuation must in effect assume that the agency would not last forever. Hence, for example, in Ramsay itself Flaux J adopted a multiplier of 4. For those reasons, I would respectfully differ from his observations, if by them, he was intending to lay down a hard and fast rule that no account whatsoever can be taken of the prospect of a termination in the future.*
>
> *[170] …. The better way, therefore, to consider rights of termination is, in my view, to say that they can be factored into account in a valuation which has to be conducted on a 'real-world' basis.*"

Similarly, in *Monk v Largo Foods Ltd*,[114] the Court held that "*The fixed term period of an agency, or the principal's desire to terminate it, are not themselves factors which reduce the compensation recoverable for loss of the agency, but the valuation which a hypothetical purchaser would ascribe to an*

114 [2016] EWHC 1837 (Comm)

agency will inevitably reflect the range of uncertainties inherent in the acquisition of such a business."

In *Green Deal Marketing Southern Limited v Economy Energy Trading Limited and others,*[115] the court plotted a path between *Ramsey* and *Software Incubator*, by finding that termination rights were relevant but that their relevance was limited, because the hypothetical purchaser has a compensation right on termination – which in effect balances out the downside of the risk of termination. To put it rhetorically, why be concerned about a risk of termination if that potential termination gives rise to the right to compensation? Indeed, a commercial agent's Regulation 17 rights could be viewed as being worth paying for. In *Green Deal Marketing* the Judge said:

> "*[156(6)] the agency in the hands of any notional purchaser would itself attract compensation rights in the event of termination. It is hard to see how the existence of a contractual termination right (including non-continuance after expiry of a fixed term) can be invoked to limit compensation when it is the fact of termination that gives rise to the entitlement to compensation. This leads me to the conclusion that, although the court is not obliged to make unrealistic assumptions about the continuation of an agency in perpetuity, the relevance of termination rights is limited. It is, however, real. A factor of obvious relevance to valuations of businesses is the uncertainty concerning future performance. The fact that an agency contract is not perpetual but can be lawfully terminated by the principal must be relevant to a realistic valuation of the agency, because it means that the principal will have a legitimate opportunity to avail himself of a get-out in the event of adverse trading conditions without the need to pay damages for breach of contract. Additionally, where compensation is not excluded by regulation 18, I see no proper reason for ignoring the fact, if it be such, that if the business were to have continued it might become liable to be terminated lawfully by the principal on account of continuing breaches of contract...*"

115 [2019] EWHC 507 (Ch)

The issue of uncertainty concerning future performance identified in *Green Deal Marketing* is a factor that would be taken account of in determining the likely future commissions, or the multiplier, and it is a very different issue from the relevance of termination rights. For example, an agency involved in supplying a principal's machinery into a coal-fired power station may have very limited future prospects and that would no doubt be reflected in the hypothetical future commissions and the multiplier.

In and of itself, it seems that the principal's contractual right to terminate should <u>not</u> affect the valuation of compensation. What must be assumed is 'proper performance' of the agency contract, which (as *Lonsdale* confirms in the part of the judgment quoted above which is underlined) means it is necessary to assume the agency would have continued.

How to calculate an indemnity

Regulation 17(3) provides (with emphasis added):

> "*… the commercial agent shall be entitled to an indemnity if and to the extent that—*
>
> *(a) he has brought the principal <u>new customers</u> or has <u>significantly increased</u> the volume of business with existing customers and the principal <u>continues to derive substantial benefits</u> from the business with such customers; and*
>
> *(b) <u>the payment of this indemnity is equitable</u> having regard to all the circumstances and, in particular, the commission lost by the commercial agent on the business transacted with such customers.*" (emphasis added).

Regulation 17(4) provides:

> *"The amount of the indemnity shall not exceed a figure equivalent to an indemnity for one year calculated from the commercial agent's average annual remuneration over the preceding five years and if the contract goes back less than five years the indemnity shall be calculated on the average for the period in question."*

Unlike the compensation provisions, there is no settled English case law that details comprehensively how the English court will calculate an indemnity. However, guidance can be found in the one reported English case dealing with an indemnity calculation (*Moore v Piretta*[116]), as well as a report prepared by the EU commission on the application of Regulation 17 (the "**Commission Report**").[117] The Commission Report looks closely to German law (from which the right to an indemnity originated), when explaining how an indemnity ought to be calculated.

There are a number of elements to Regulation 17(3) that are to be taken into account in the calculation of the indemnity and these are considered below.

New customers and increased business with existing customers

Regulation 17(3) provides that an assessment needs to be undertaken of:

1. The number of new customers brought to the principal by the agent; and

2. The extent to which the agent has "*significantly increased the volume of business with existing customers*".

There is no definition of "*significant increase*" in the Regulations and this issue has not been considered by the English court.

It is likely that the English courts will look at each case on its own facts. Certainly, it is likely that if there were two customers at the outset of the agency each doing £1 million of business with the principal, and the agent persuaded each to increase purchases by £500,000 (adding £1 million to the value of the overall sales), the courts would hold that 'significant' increases had been achieved.

In respect of new customers, the Commission Report states that a small level of involvement from the agent is all that is required in acquiring the new customer in order for them to be included in the indemnity calculation, and suggests that "*it is enough merely that the agent contributed*

116 [1998] CLC 992

117 Report on the Application of Article 17 of Council Directive on the Co-ordination of the Laws of Member States relating to Self-Employed Commercial Agents (86/653/EEC) (Com (96) 314 final).

in bringing the new customer". The English court in *Moore v Piretta* agreed with this analysis.

Continues to derive substantial benefits

Regulation 17(3)(a) provides that "... *the commercial agent shall be entitled to an indemnity if and to the extent that the principal continues to derive substantial benefits from the business*" with new customers or customers with whom the agent has significantly increased the volume of business.

This will lead to an assessment of how long it is considered that the new business introduced by the agent, or the business with customers with whom the agent has substantially increased the volume of sales, will last. The Commission Report states that the usual approach in Germany is 2 to 3 years but it may be as much as 5 years. There seems no reason in principle to apply a 'tariff' approach; the English courts are much more likely to consider the relevant period in each case based on the specific facts of that case – and that period might well be shorter or longer than the period normally applied in German cases.

In addition, a "migration" factor will be applied to the calculation, to take account of the fact that over the course of time customers will naturally move away from a principal. This is calculated as a percentage of commission on a per annum basis, and can be as high as almost 40%, according to the Commission Report.

A further reduction of around 10% is then applied to take account of the fact that the agent is receiving accelerated payment.

Payment of indemnity must be equitable

As noted above, Regulation 17(3)(b) provides that *the commercial agent shall be entitled to an indemnity if and to the extent that the payment of this indemnity is equitable having regard to all the circumstances and, in particular, the commission lost by the commercial agent on the business transacted with such customers*".

The commission report states that the indemnity figure is rarely adjusted for reasons of equity in practice, though it goes on to list a number of factors which may be taken into account.

A key issue in this respect is "*the fault of the agent*". In this respect, if the court finds that the agent has breached the contract, but that those breaches are not so serious as to deprive it of the right to an indemnity, it is something that the court may use to reduce the level of the indemnity. The European Court of Justice held this was likely to be the case in *Volvo Car Germany GmbH v Autohof Wiedensdorf GmbH*[118] in which the court held: "*The possibility cannot, therefore, be ruled out that that agent's conduct may be taken into account in the assessment made to determine the fairness of his indemnity*".

Other factors identified in the Commission Report to be of relevance as to whether the payment of the indemnity is equitable are:

1. If the agent is retained by other principals.

   The Commission Report states that if the agent continues to service the same customers post-termination, but for a different principal, the agent will have no right to an indemnity. However, the Report also states that whether an agent is retained by other principals is relevant in calculating the indemnity. The report does not amplify the point and it would seem unfair if the agent lost its entitlement to an indemnity if, for example, it sold different products on behalf of other principals.

2. *"The level of remuneration of the agent. For example, did the principal recently reduce the rate of commission e.g. because he felt that agent's earnings were becoming too high or pay to the agent a large amount of commission on contracts with customers which the agent did not introduce or had little to do with? Also, did the agent receive special compensation for keeping a consignment inventory, special bonuses for new clients, del credere commission, any special allowance for trade fairs or extra payments for sub-agents? Did he incur costs regarding loss of sub-agents?"*

3. Decrease in turnover of the principal.

4. Extent of the advantage to the principal.

118 Case C/203-09

5. Payment of pension contributions by the principal.
6. *"The existence of restraint of trade clauses. Clearly, a principal will be required to pay a higher indemnity for this."*

Cap

Regulation 17(4) is a statutory cap on the amount of the indemnity and is a "*final corrective*" rather than the starting point.[119] If the steps referred to above result in an indemnity which is higher than the agent's annual average commissions over the last five years (or less if the agency is less than 5 years old), then the indemnity will be in the sum of the agent's annual average commissions over the relevant period.[120] If the indemnity calculation is lower than the cap, the lower sum will be payable.

Summary of the likely indemnity calculation

Whilst the approach that the court will adopt to calculating an indemnity is not settled, it is likely that the following steps will be followed (as broadly set out in the Commission Report):

1. The number of new customers brought to the principal by the agent will be assessed, as will the extent to which the agent has "*significantly increased the volume of business with existing customers*".
2. Once step 1 has been completed, the commission paid in respect of these customers would be calculated for the last 12 months of the contract (less expenses incurred by the agents in generating that commission).
3. An estimate (expressed in terms of years) then needs to be made as to the future duration of the benefits to the principal deriving from the business with the customers identified at 1 and 2 above. This will be customer, market and sector specific, though as

119 According to the Commission Report

120 This was what happened in *Moore v Piretta*; the calculation resulted at £92,000, so the cap of £64,526.33 was awarded to the agent.

noted above, the Commission Report states that 2-3 years is considered a normal period in Germany.

4. In addition, the court will apply a "migration" factor to the calculation, to take account of the fact that over the course of time customers will naturally move away from a principal. This is calculated as a percentage of commission on a per annum basis, and can be as high as 40% (according to the Commission Report).

5. A further reduction is then applied to take account of the fact that the agent is receiving accelerated payment.

6. The question of equity is then considered and the figure arrived at under steps 1 to 5 is adjusted. Factors such as restraint of trade clauses can increase the payment, whereas the agent's conduct can reduce the payment.

7. The cap is then calculated by taking an average of the commissions paid over the last 5 years. If the amount arrived at under 1-6 above is less than the cap, the sum calculated under 1-6 is awarded. If the sum calculated under 1-6 above is more than the cap, the capped figure is awarded.

MORE BOOKS BY LAW BRIEF PUBLISHING

A selection of our other titles available now:-

'Covid-19, Homeworking and the Law – The Essential Guide to Employment and GDPR Issues' by Forbes Solicitors
'Covid-19, Force Majeure and Frustration of Contracts – The Essential Guide' by Keith Markham
'Covid-19 and Criminal Law – The Essential Guide' by Ramya Nagesh
'Covid-19 and Family Law in England and Wales – The Essential Guide' by Safda Mahmood
'Covid-19 and the Implications for Planning Law – The Essential Guide' by Bob Mc Geady & Meyric Lewis
'Covid-19, Residential Property, Equity Release and Enfranchisement – The Essential Guide' by Paul Sams and Louise Uphill
'Covid-19, Brexit and the Law of Commercial Leases – The Essential Guide' by Mark Shelton
'Covid-19 and the Law Relating to Food in the UK and Republic of Ireland – The Essential Guide' by Ian Thomas
'A Practical Guide to the General Data Protection Regulation (GDPR) – 2nd Edition' by Keith Markham
'Ellis on Credit Hire – Sixth Edition' by Aidan Ellis & Tim Kevan
'A Practical Guide to Working with Litigants in Person and McKenzie Friends in Family Cases' by Stuart Barlow
'Protecting Unregistered Brands: A Practical Guide to the Law of Passing Off' by Lorna Brazell
'A Practical Guide to Secondary Liability and Joint Enterprise Post-Jogee' by Joanne Cecil & James Mehigan

'A Practical Guide to the Pre-Action RTA Claims Protocol for Personal Injury Lawyers' by Antonia Ford
'A Practical Guide to Neighbour Disputes and the Law' by Alexander Walsh
'A Practical Guide to Forfeiture of Leases' by Mark Shelton
'A Practical Guide to Coercive Control for Legal Practitioners and Victims' by Rachel Horman
'A Practical Guide to Rights Over Airspace and Subsoil' by Daniel Gatty
'Tackling Disclosure in the Criminal Courts – A Practitioner's Guide' by Narita Bahra QC & Don Ramble
'A Practical Guide to the Law of Driverless Cars – Second Edition' by Alex Glassbrook, Emma Northey & Scarlett Milligan
'A Practical Guide to TOLATA Claims' by Greg Williams
'Artificial Intelligence – The Practical Legal Issues' by John Buyers
'A Practical Guide to the Law of Prescription in Scotland' by Andrew Foyle
'A Practical Guide to the Construction and Rectification of Wills and Trust Instruments' by Edward Hewitt
'A Practical Guide to the Law of Bullying and Harassment in the Workplace' by Philip Hyland
'How to Be a Freelance Solicitor: A Practical Guide to the SRA-Regulated Freelance Solicitor Model' by Paul Bennett
'A Practical Guide to Prison Injury Claims' by Malcolm Johnson
'A Practical Guide to the Small Claims Track' by Dominic Bright
'A Practical Guide to Advising Clients at the Police Station' by Colin Stephen McKeown-Beaumont
'A Practical Guide to Antisocial Behaviour Injunctions' by Iain Wightwick
'Practical Mediation: A Guide for Mediators, Advocates, Advisers, Lawyers, and Students in Civil, Commercial, Business, Property, Workplace, and Employment Cases' by Jonathan Dingle with John Sephton
'The Mini-Pupillage Workbook' by David Boyle

'A Practical Guide to Crofting Law' by Brian Inkster
'A Practical Guide to Spousal Maintenance' by Liz Cowell
'A Practical Guide to the Law of Domain Names and Cybersquatting' by Andrew Clemson
'A Practical Guide to the Law of Gender Pay Gap Reporting' by Harini Iyengar
'A Practical Guide to the Rights of Grandparents in Children Proceedings' by Stuart Barlow
'NHS Whistleblowing and the Law' by Joseph England
'Employment Law and the Gig Economy' by Nigel Mackay & Annie Powell
'A Practical Guide to Noise Induced Hearing Loss (NIHL) Claims' by Andrew Mckie, Ian Skeate, Gareth McAloon
'An Introduction to Beauty Negligence Claims – A Practical Guide for the Personal Injury Practitioner' by Greg Almond
'Intercompany Agreements for Transfer Pricing Compliance' by Paul Sutton
'Zen and the Art of Mediation' by Martin Plowman
'A Practical Guide to the SRA Principles, Individual and Law Firm Codes of Conduct 2019 – What Every Law Firm Needs to Know' by Paul Bennett
'A Practical Guide to Adoption for Family Lawyers' by Graham Pegg
'A Practical Guide to Industrial Disease Claims' by Andrew Mckie & Ian Skeate
'A Practical Guide to Redundancy' by Philip Hyland
'A Practical Guide to Vicarious Liability' by Mariel Irvine
'A Practical Guide to Applications for Landlord's Consent and Variation of Leases' by Mark Shelton
'A Practical Guide to Relief from Sanctions Post-Mitchell and Denton' by Peter Causton
'A Practical Guide to Equity Release for Advisors' by Paul Sams
'A Practical Guide to Unlawful Eviction and Harassment' by Stephanie Lovegrove
'A Practical Guide to the Law Relating to Food' by Ian Thomas

'A Practical Guide to Financial Services Claims' by Chris Hegarty
'The Law of Houses in Multiple Occupation: A Practical Guide to HMO Proceedings' by Julian Hunt
'A Practical Guide to Unlawful Eviction and Harassment' by Stephanie Lovegrove
'A Practical Guide to Solicitor and Client Costs' by Robin Dunne
'Occupiers, Highways and Defective Premises Claims: A Practical Guide Post-Jackson – 2nd Edition' by Andrew Mckie
'A Practical Guide to Financial Ombudsman Service Claims' by Adam Temple & Robert Scrivenor
'A Practical Guide to Advising Schools on Employment Law' by Jonathan Holden
'A Practical Guide to Running Housing Disrepair and Cavity Wall Claims: 2nd Edition' by Andrew Mckie & Ian Skeate
'A Practical Guide to Holiday Sickness Claims – 2nd Edition' by Andrew Mckie & Ian Skeate
'Arguments and Tactics for Personal Injury and Clinical Negligence Claims' by Dorian Williams
'A Practical Guide to QOCS and Fundamental Dishonesty' by James Bentley
'A Practical Guide to Drone Law' by Rufus Ballaster, Andrew Firman, Eleanor Clot
'A Practical Guide to Compliance for Personal Injury Firms Working With Claims Management Companies' by Paul Bennett
'A Practical Guide to the Landlord and Tenant Act 1954: Commercial Tenancies' by Richard Hayes & David Sawtell
'A Practical Guide to Dog Law for Owners and Others' by Andrea Pitt
'RTA Allegations of Fraud in a Post-Jackson Era: The Handbook – 2nd Edition' by Andrew Mckie
'RTA Personal Injury Claims: A Practical Guide Post-Jackson' by Andrew Mckie
'On Experts: CPR35 for Lawyers and Experts' by David Boyle
'An Introduction to Personal Injury Law' by David Boyle

'A Practical Guide to Chronic Pain Claims' by Pankaj Madan
'A Practical Guide to Claims Arising from Fatal Accidents' by James Patience
'A Practical Guide to Subtle Brain Injury Claims' by Pankaj Madan

www.ingramcontent.com/pod-product-compliance
Lightning Source LLC
LaVergne TN
LVHW022052200926
848481LV00003B/881
* 9 7 8 1 9 1 3 7 1 5 6 4 9 *